A JOURNAL
on FRIENDSHIP

AN INTERACTIVE
FRIEND-TO-FRIEND JOURNAL

KIMBERLY KIRBERGER

Chicken Soup for the Teenage Soul *series*

Health Communications, Inc.
Deerfield Beach, Florida

www.hci-online.com
www.love4teens.com

We would like to acknowledge the many publishers and individuals who granted us permission to reprint the cited material. (Note: The stories that were penned anonymously, that are in the public domain, or that were written by Kimberly Kirberger are not included in this listing.)

Junior High from a High-School Perspective and *Making a Difference*. Reprinted by permission of Allison Thorp. ©2001 Allison Thorp.

Be Yourself. Reprinted by permission of Lisa McDonald. ©2000 Lisa McDonald.

From the Inside Out and *Clouded Memory*. Reprinted by permission of Anne G. Fegely. ©2001 Anne G. Fegely.

Seeing My Inner Self. Reprinted by permission of Kristina Hardenbrook. ©2001 Kristina Hardenbrook.

She. Reprinted by permission of Jennie Christine Petkis. ©2001 Jennie Christine Petkis.

Still Standing. Reprinted by permission of Sara Beth Cowan. ©2001 Sara Beth Cowan.

My Greatest Friend. Reprinted by permission of Megan Kimm Snook. ©2000 Megan Kimm Snook.

A True Friend. Reprinted by permission of Candace Schoonhoven. ©2000 Candace Schoonhoven.

(Continued on page 357)

©2001 Kimberly Kirberger
ISBN 1-55874-912-8

Publisher: Health Communications, Inc.
       3201 S.W. 15th Street
       Deerfield Beach, FL 33442-8190

Cover and inside book design by Lawna Patterson Oldfield

With love, I dedicate this journal:

To Jesse, my best friend and favorite person.
I love you so much.

To my dear friends, Lia, Tasha and Colin.
You bring lots of happiness and
laughter to my life.

To Christine, Nico, Jenny, Hayley and Ashley,
and all the teenagers who inspire me
and make this world a much funner place to be.

Contents

Acknowledgments xiii
Introduction xvii
Friendship Is xix

1. Being Yourself
Being Yourself 3
Junior High from a
   High-School Perspective *Allison Thorp* 5
Be Yourself *Lisa McDonald* 11
From the Inside Out *Anne G. Fegely* 13
Dear Friend 15
Best Friend's Pages 16
Think About It 19
Seeing My Inner Self *Kristina Hardenbrook* 20
She *Jennie Christine Petkis* 26

2. Being Your Own Best Friend
Being Your Own Best Friend 39
Still Standing *Sara Beth Cowan* 41
Dear Friend 49
Best Friend's Pages 50
Think About It 55
My Greatest Friend *Megan Kimm Snook* 59

3. What Is Friendship?

What Is Friendship? 69

A True Friend   *Candace Schoonhoven* 71

A.K.A. Friend   *Jessica Cox* 76

Dear Friend 77

Best Friend's Pages 78

The Oath of a True Friend   *Alejandra Capdevila* 80

Think About It 81

4. Challenges in Friendship

Challenges in Friendship 101

Dear Friend 103

Best Friend's Pages 104

Think About It 106

5. Making Friends

Making Friends 123

Rose   *Christi Bergschneider* 124

Dear Friend 129

Best Friend's Pages 130

Clouded Memory   *Anne G. Fegely* 133

Think About It 134

6. Cliques, Groups and Popularity

Cliques, Groups and Popularity 151

Dear Friend 162

Best Friend's Pages 163

Think About It 165

Tables Turned   *Leah Houston* 168

7. Friends and Lovers

Friends and Lovers 179

Dear Friend 185

Best Friend's Pages 186

Think About It 189

My Friend   *Rebecca Woolf* 190

My Heart   *Miranda Karkling* 196

8. Jealousy, Hurt and Betrayal

Jealousy, Hurt and Betrayal 207

Friends   *Michele Booths* 210

Dear Friend 225

Best Friend's Pages 226

Think About It 229

Lullaby for Your Friend   *Rebecca Woolf* 231

Her   *Sami Armin* 236

9. Friends in Trouble

Friends in Trouble 247

The Night   *Jennifer Phillips* 249

My Friends   *Eric Solan* 260

Dear Friend 261

Best Friend's Pages 262

Think About It 265

The Walk   *Elizabeth Waisanen* 272

10. Growing Apart

Growing Apart 281

Freefall   *Julie McKeon* 285

Dear Friend 287

Best Friend's Pages 288

Think About It 290

Childhood Memories   *Holly Hoffman* 293

11. The Best of Friendship

The Best of Friendship 305

I Found a Tiny Starfish   *Dayle Ann Dodds* 308

My Perfect Friend   *Tasha Boucher* 311

Dear Friend 317

Best Friend's Pages 318

Think About It 320

The One You Rely On   *Jesse Patrick* 323

Lessons from Friends   *Jenny Sharaf* 329

My Best Friend   *Teal Henderson* 334

Making a Difference   *Allison Thorp* 336

The Best Advice   *Teal Henderson* 338

My Wish for You   *Emily Kaiser* 342

Who Is Kimberly Kirberger? 349

Contributors 351

Permissions *(continued)* 357

Acknowledgments

This journal is a continuation of the book *Teen Love: On Friendship* and was compiled and written with the help of some very special people. I love having the opportunity to express my gratitude for their contributions and friendship.

First and foremost, I want to thank my son, Jesse, who always inspires me to do my best, to be honest and to be myself. He embodies these traits totally. He is loyal, funny, smart and the best person I know.

I want to thank my brother, Jack, for always believing in me and supporting me. All the work you have done for teens has rubbed off on me and inspired me to be better at what I do. Most of all, I want to thank you for who you are, the love we share, for being a true brother, and for supporting me in a way that feels magical. When you say, "YOU can do it," I truly believe I can.

I want to thank my husband for the moments he makes me laugh and the important lessons he has taught me about friendship.

I want to thank Christine, Jenny and Hayley, the teens who worked tirelessly on this journal. They made a huge contribution, both by choosing many of the poems and by writing many of the questions. I love you guys and I am so pleased with the quality of the work you do and the work you did for this book. Thank you, Christine, for your calm and loving kindness. Thank you, Hayley, for your quick mind and your beautiful heart. And thank you, Jenny, for your ongoing commitment and your incredibly sharp writing skills. You guys played a really big part in creating this journal.

Tasha, I love that I get to thank you in printed words. I love that you will have these words to look at whenever you need to know how much you are loved and how much you are appreciated. We have become such a good team that I can't really separate what I do from what you do. You always sneak in a word or change a sentence just so I will look like I know what I am doing. You are very generous in that way: generous with your heart, your energy and your spirit. I thank you all the time in my heart and these words barely come close to the gratitude I feel.

Mitch, I feel the same for you. You do so much and contribute so much that things get done without me ever having to worry about them. You care about everything being done right and you don't stop until it is. I respect you so much, Mitch. Your integrity, loyalty and friendship make me feel incredibly honored to work with you. These are just a few of the qualities that I have come to depend on you for and couldn't continue without.

Lisa, you have become a friend as well as a wonderful assistant, and I am very happy about both. I love your positive attitude, and I think it is an incredible attribute to always see the good in things. You are a pleasure to work with, and you make everyone's day better by just being you. Thanks for everything.

Nina continues to keep the office going, the Teen Letter

Project going and the heart of I.A.M. 4 Teens going. I love how much you care about teenagers and teachers who work with teenagers. Thanks so much for all you do and continue to do for us and for teens.

Kelly Harrington, thank you for your hard work in acquiring the permissions for this book and all the research you do in locating poetry for this and other books. It has been a great pleasure to work with you.

I want to thank Sharon House for getting the message out there about these books. Your support and hard work mean so much to me, and I know that you share my passion for helping teens. You are a very important part of our team, and I appreciate you more than words can say. You are a talented publicist and a trusted colleague.

Lisa Drucker and Susan Tobias are my talented editors at Health Communications, Inc. I don't know what I would do without the two of you. You make my life so much easier with your collective patience and sweetness. You both have such a loving way of infusing each and every message, e-mail or conversation with care and support. I feel blessed to be able to work with you two. Thank you for all you have done for me and for this journal.

Lawna Patterson Oldfield did an excellent job on the graphics for this book. I greatly appreciate the creativity and energy that you put into this project. The care you took to find just the right images for each section meant so much to me. You are a gifted artist, and I thank you for putting your talent to work in the pages of this journal.

As always, Kim Weiss, you have done a wonderful job on the publicity for this book. You are a joy to work with and a pleasure to know, Kim. Thanks for your support, your laughter and your continuing friendship.

A hearty thank-you to Terry Burke and his sales team and Kelly Maragni and her marketing team at Health Communications, Inc. Thank you so much for making sure the *Teen Love* series gets into the hands of teenagers all over the country and the world.

Peter Vegso, thank you for continuing to believe in the work I do for teens.

I want to extend a special thanks to Seth Epstein, Rich Kaylor and Matt Marquis for their work on the commercial for *Teen Love: On Friendship*. Thanks for the hard work, the amazing creativity and the very cool content.

Thanks to Lia for giving me the kind of friendship that just gets better and better. You are so dear to me and always will be.

And last, but not least, thanks to Colin for your friendship, support and dedication to helping teens. I am really glad we get to work together.

# Introduction

Dear Teen,

If someone told you that they knew of a way that you could understand yourself better, develop inner security, become a happier person, like yourself more, be a better friend and possess an all-around more positive attitude in 5-20 minutes a day, would you be interested?

Journaling can achieve these things and it only requires a little bit of your time and your honesty.

I receive hundreds of letters a day from teenagers like you (in fact one could have actually been from you) and some of the most profound ones are in response to the two journals I have compiled. I hear from teenagers who swear that their lives have changed completely because of the time they spent answering questions, reflecting on who they are and having the courage to go deep and discover their true selves. I hear over and over again that their self-worth and self-love increased greatly as a result of completing their journals.

This journal starts with "Being Yourself" and takes you through challenges in friendship, making friends, hurt, betrayal, jealousy, cliques, groups and popularity. It then deals with the hardest part of friendship: friends in trouble. So that we could finish up on a positive note we end with a celebration of friendship in the chapter "The Best of Friendship."

My favorite thing about this journal is that in each chapter we have the "Best Friend's Pages." This is a section that your closest friend will fill out. I suggest that you give your friend the journal to fill out BEFORE you begin to do your part. Ideally you will both have a journal and be able to fill out each other's "Best Friend's Pages" before filling out your own.

When you are filling out your own pages you will encounter some challenging moments. You will be asked to remember some difficult and painful experiences. The importance of working your way through these questions is that each time you are willing to face your pain and examine a painful experience, you can then truly put it behind you. There are also many questions that will help you to understand what kind of friend you are and the nature of the friends you choose. For most people these are questions that will bring back both happy and sad moments. You will be examining yourself and looking at what is important to you. As I have said many times, the better you know yourself, the better off you will be in all areas of your life.

It is my deepest hope that this journal will help you to see and understand the importance of friends. I also hope it will remind you that as humans we all make mistakes, we all misjudge people and we all need to learn to be more forgiving of our friends and of ourselves.

Learning to be a good friend is a process and we are constantly faced with opportunities to practice what we learn along the way. I hope that this journal will provide you with the guidance needed to get to know yourself better and to appreciate this amazing thing called friendship.

Friendship Is . . .

On our Web site I posted the following questions about friendship. This is a small sampling of the answers. I want to thank all of you who took the time to respond to my questions.

What makes you mad at your best friend?

- When she breaks promises.
- When she ignores me, or doesn't fill me in on plans.
- When she doesn't call back, or breaks our plans to go out with her boyfriend.
- When I'm ignored. Actually, that makes me more hurt than mad.

What makes you mad in general?

- Close-minded people.
- Liars! I just don't like people who lie.
- People who are mean. People who think they know everything.

What is the nicest thing you have ever done for a friend?

- Helped someone with their schoolwork.
- I think that the nicest thing a person can do for another person is to really listen to them when they need someone to listen to them.

- In eighth grade I liked this guy who liked my friend, and I told her I didn't like him anymore so that she would date him. I knew if she knew I did like him, she wouldn't have gone out with him. I try to do nice things every day.

What is the meanest thing you have ever done to a friend?

- I told my best friend I hated her and never wanted to see her again when we were fighting. I regret it because I said it out of anger and I didn't mean it, and I'm sure it's hard for her to forget that I said it.
- Talk about her behind her back.
- Lied to her.
- I am still really good friends with my ex-boyfriend, Kyle. We had been dating on and off for five months when one day I just got bored and broke things off out of the blue. It really hurt him. Luckily we are still friends.

What is the nicest thing a friend has done for you?

- My best friend has always been there to give me advice, and she's helped me come out of my "shell." Now I'm not nearly as shy as I used to be.
- I was in an accident and the guy who was with me sat with me and bought me a teddy bear just to show he cared.
- Try to help me realize that I wasn't alone in the world.
- Didn't exclude me.
- For my birthday, my friend Kyle filled my room with roses and daisies (my favorite flowers) and made me a little "Story of Us" book. It was so sweet.
- Listen to me complain and help me solve my problems.

What is the meanest thing a friend has done to you?

- Talked about me behind my back.
- Ignored me and talked about me behind my back.
- My (ex) friend was always talking about me behind my back to my other friends. She had something against me and tried to turn all of my other friends against me. It kind of split my group of friends in half.

What do you want to know about your friends?

- The one thing they look for most out of life.
- If they really hurt as much on the inside as I do.

What do you want your friends to know about you?

- That I want nothing more than to be a strong person. I also want them to know that I put on a good mask because I'm very seldom truly happy. What I want most out of life is to be truly happy, but I don't know what I need that will make me happy.
- Who I really am and not the person I pretend to be.
- That I make mistakes.
- That I love them and I'd do anything for them.

What do you look for in a friend?

- Someone who will be there for me through thick and thin; someone who is honest and caring; someone who I can tell my deepest secrets to; someone who's not afraid to tell me their deepest secrets; someone who has a good sense of humor; someone who has goals; someone who will just listen to me without judging me.

- Someone who is honest, fun to be with, who likes me for me and can take the good with the bad.
- Someone who is nice and understanding.
- A good listener!
- Someone honest, not completely self-involved and fun.
- Someone who is trustworthy, loyal, kind, fun to be with, funny, not really ditzy, a good listener and someone who likes me for me.

If you could change one thing about friendship, what would it be?

- Make it more open emotionally. If someone has a problem, it can get taken care of more quickly and easily.
- Make it last forever so that you never get hurt.
- Make people be honest, so friendships would not be messed up.
- Have no hurt feelings ever!

one

When you hold fast to your beliefs and

live true to yourself, your real value

as a human being shines through.

Daisaku Ikeda

Being Yourself

It just seems like you agree
to have a certain personality or something.
For no reason. Just to make things easier for
everyone. But when you think about it,
I mean, how do you know it's even you?

Angela
My So-Called Life

Have you ever met someone who was totally at ease and comfortable with themselves? Have you ever had days where you felt really good about yourself and because of that it seemed like everyone else responded to you in a positive way? There is a vibe people give off when they feel good about themselves. It is hard to explain but it is unmistakable when someone has it.

And there is also the other side of this. We have all had days where we felt unattractive. We would try to cover up our insecurity and act like everything was okay but no matter how hard we tried, it seemed the discomfort we felt was obvious to everyone we came in contact with.

The difference between the two experiences is simple. When we know who we are and accept who we are, we have real security. We are comfortable with ourselves and that comfort allows for genuine happiness. Not only are we happy with ourselves, but other people are happy to be around us.

We all want to enjoy this security and that is why the work we do to get to know ourselves better is so important. Getting to know yourself and liking yourself is one of the most important things you will ever do. As you answer the questions in this chapter, be aware of any temptation you have to stray from your true self. Remember that what makes each person special is not only the positive traits they possess, but also their quirks. Remember to have fun with this while understanding its importance. With each question you answer you are getting closer to knowing who you are. As you get to truly know yourself, you will also begin to like what you see. I wish you the very best on this most important journey.

Junior High from a High-School Perspective

Isn't it amazing?
That a place which once caused such
    angst,
Such isolation
And seclusion
Can now provide such insight
And reflection
To the days when we knew all
Yet we knew nothing.

It used to be I
Who, inadequate as I was,
Sat alone and longed to be
Everything I could not.
I thought the world revolved
Around what I did not have:
Money, beauty, power.
And perhaps a portion of it does,
Still a greater portion of it doesn't.
I longed so long to be beautiful
I didn't realize I already was
In my own special way.

And now that the years have passed
    by,
I realize everyone has their own little
    insecurities.

Imagination kicks back,
And reality sets in.
People don't need another pretty
　　face.
They need an open heart,
A listening ear,
An encouraging word.
How shallow seem now
The popular "heroes" I so foolishly
　　idolized.
The friend I held in such high esteem
Was the same one who tore me down.
I thought her to be so perfect
And set her as the prototype
I wanted to be.
Only now do I realize
All the time I spent wishing I was
　　someone else
That someone else was wishing they
　　were me.
Such wasted time we spent
Seeking out lives that were not our own.
Years later when the boys are all
　　grown,
And our clothes out of date,
Upon which memories will we truly
　look back and smile?
I think they will be
The ones when we became ourselves.

Allison Thorp

Being Yourself

★ What unique characteristics do you possess?

1. _____
2. _____
3. _____
4. _____
5. _____

★ What makes you special?

1. _____
2. _____
3. _____
4. _____
5. _____

★ What do you admire most about yourself?

1. _____
2. _____
3. _____
4. _____

5. _____

6. _____

7. _____

8. _____

9. _____

★ What values are important to you? Define what each of these mean to you and how important they are to you:

✓ Trust: _____

_____

_____

✓ Self-Discipline: _____

_____

_____

✓ Charity: _____

_____

_____

✓ Honesty: _____

_____

_____

✓ Humility: _____

_____

_____

✓ Respect: _____

_____

_____

✓ Responsibility: _____

_____

_____

✓ Tolerance: _____

_____

_____

✓ Compassion: _____

_____

_____

✓ Generosity: _____

_____

_____

★ Do you feel you are true to yourself? Give one example:

_____

_____

_____

_____

_____

_____

_____

★ Do you ever change how you act depending on the people you are around? Give an example:

_____

_____

_____

_____

_____

_____

_____

_____

Be Yourself

Sometimes it's best not to follow the crowd,
Because when you are yourself, you always feel proud.

Instead of things most people seek,
Create your own and be unique.

When it's cool to go left, veer to the right,
When all the colors are dull, be the one that's bright.

When it's hip to be striped, decide to be plaid,
Yearn to be good while all else is bad.

Stand up straight while the world slouches down,
Offer a smile when all you see are frowns.

It's easy to do, to be one of a kind,
Ignore the insults, practice being kind.

Be yourself, it's the right thing to do,
It's the only way to get to know *you*.

Lisa McDonald

★ Put these character traits in the order you feel is most important:

____	Honesty	____	Punctuality
____	Responsibility	____	Compassion
____	Kindness	____	Integrity
____	Creativity	____	Wisdom
____	Strength	____	Loyalty
____	Courage	____	Sincerity
____	Humility	____	Originality

★ Write a paragraph and describe yourself physically:

For example:

I am 5'5" and weigh 120 lbs. I have brown hair, etc.

_____

_____

_____

_____

_____

_____

_____

_____

★ Write a paragraph that describes your personality:

_____

_____

_____

_____

_____

From the Inside Out

If people were seen
From the inside out,
Kings might be
Paupers of the soul.
And wealthy be
The hearts of the poor
Homely be the faces
Of the proud
And beautiful be
Those we overlook.
If we could see
Inside ourselves,
We might be
Beside ourselves
If we learned to love
From the inside out.

Anne G. Fegely

What is your favorite:

TV show: _____

Movie: _____

Book: _____

Color: _____

Music: _____

Piece of clothing: _____

Pair of shoes: _____

Thing to do with your friends: _____

_____

Magazine: _____

Who is your favorite:

Relative:_____   Politician: _____

Friend:_____   Religious figure: _____

Actor:_____   Person who isn't a friend: ___

Actress: _____   _____

Teacher:_____   Singer: _____

Sports figure: _____   Parent of a friend: _____

Younger person: _____   Role model: _____

Dear Friend

Included in each chapter of this journal are "Best Friend's Pages." These are questions for your best friend to answer about you and about your friendship. We recommend that your friend fill these out before you begin the journaling process. This is important because you will want to turn to these pages for support when you are faced with a difficult question or memory. Also, you will find great strength and wisdom in seeing yourself through your friend's eyes.

In each chapter you will have the opportunity to write a letter to your friend at the beginning of his or her pages. For this chapter, tell your best friend what it means to you to have him or her in your life and what it will mean to you to have these pages:

Dear _____,

_____

_____

_____

_____

_____

_____

_____

Best Friend's Pages

★ When was the first time you saw the real me or felt like you really knew and understood me?

_____

_____

_____

_____

_____

★ Do you feel you know the real me? Why or why not?

_____

_____

_____

_____

★ What do you respect most about me?

_____

_____

_____

_____

★ What five words would you use to describe me to someone who didn't know me?

1. _____

2. _____

3. _____

4. _____

5. _____

★ Can you recall a time when I stood up for myself? How did I do that?

_____

_____

_____

_____

_____

★ What do you think is important to me? List five things:

1. _____

2. _____

3. _____

4. _____

5. _____

★ Do you feel free to be yourself when you are with me?

_____

_____

_____

_____

_____

_____

_____

? ?

★ Do I support you to be yourself? In what ways?

_____

_____

_____

_____

_____

_____

_____

Each chapter of this journal ends with a section called "Think About It." These are questions that are intended to generate a deeper questioning and understanding of yourself and your friendships. You should take your time answering these questions and only answer one at each sitting.

These pages can be done with your best friend, also. It would be fun and helpful to get into having discussions that are self-reflective rather than what we are *all* tempted to do, which is to have profound discussions about *other* people's lives. This, of course, does nothing to make us better people.

Take your time, be honest with yourself and remember, most importantly, to be kind to yourself. If you haven't thought of yourself as a friend until now, this is the perfect time to begin.

Enjoy.

In order to be the best version of ourselves that we can be, it is important to take the time to get to know ourselves. When we answer questions like the ones in this chapter, we begin to define who we are. Once we begin to understand ourselves better, we can let our true selves out to play. With self-knowledge, we bring more richness and depth to our friendships. We simply have more to offer.

Enjoy taking the time to get to know yourself in these pages.

Seeing My Inner Self

It glistens when the sun hits it
And makes light shapes on my walls.
They only stay for a little bit.
Bad luck for years if it falls.

It tells me "wash your face,"
Or "do your hair."
Sometimes I stand there in front of it
And can't help but only stare.

It tells me if I'm very plain,
It points out if I'm a cutie.
I can't help if at times I complain,
Because it doesn't show my inner beauty.

Kristina Hardenbrook

What Do You See
When You Look in the Mirror?

★ Make a list of the words you use to describe yourself:

1. _____

2. _____

3. _____

4. _____

5. _____

6. _____

7. _____

8. _____

9. _____

10. _____

Things are getting to me. Just how people are.
How they always expect you to be a
certain way, even your best friend.

Angela
My So-Called Life

★ Do your friends expect you to be a certain way? If so, describe how:

_____

_____

_____

_____

Listen, Pacey. If I'm thanking you
for anything . . . it's for being yourself.
It's for not caring what anybody else thinks.
It's for knowing in your heart what's wrong and
what's right. And it's for being there this
year . . . when I needed you most.

Joey
Dawson's Creek

★ Do you have any friends who you think of this way? If so, who?

_____

_____

_____

_____

★ Describe a time you did your best and you felt really good inside:

_____

_____

_____

_____

All that matters is if you can look in the mirror and honestly tell the person you see there, that you've done your best.

John McKay

★ Do you agree with this quote?   ☐ Yes   ☐ No

★ Do you usually do your best?   ☐ Yes   ☐ No

Make a promise to yourself that you will always try to do your best.

*Sometimes we get so caught up
in wanting to be liked that we hang out
with people who pull us down.*

Amanda Ford

★ Have you ever befriended people whom you knew were bad for you or who didn't really care about you? Describe the situation:

_____

_____

_____

_____

★ How did it feel?

_____

_____

★ What ended up happening?

_____

_____

_____

Accept yourself as you are.
Otherwise you will never see opportunity.
You will not feel free to move toward it;
you will feel you are not deserving.

Maxwell Maltz

*T*his is *so true!* I have learned that life gives you what you *think* you deserve.

★ List some dreams and goals that you have for yourself. Next to each one check *yes* or *no* to indicate which ones you think you deserve. If you check *no,* explain why and then do what it takes to change it to a *yes.*

☐ Yes ☐ No _____

☐ Yes ☐ No _____

☐ Yes ☐ No _____

☐ Yes ☐ No _____

☐ Yes ☐ No _____

☐ Yes ☐ No _____

☐ Yes ☐ No _____

She

The night is black all around me
swirling darkness that surrounds me.
What is this creature that I see
with bright glowing eyes that puncture me?
It is She.

She sees into my soul with piercing eyes
On the outside she laughs, on the inside she cries.
The more people want to find her
the more that she hides.
She is just like me.
It is She.

Who is this girl, covered by make-up and clothes,
thinking that a smile will hide her aching soul?
It is my reflection.
She is just like me.
She is me.
I am She.

Jennie Christine Petkis

It's like, there's this person that you want to be for other people. To make them happy. To make them proud of you. And then there's yourself. And sometimes it's hard to tell where one ends and the other begins.

Joey
Dawson's Creek

★ Do you ever feel this way? Give an example:

_____

_____

_____

★ Describe the person you are to other people:

_____

_____

_____

★ Describe the person you are inside:

_____

_____

_____

We all have times when we feel that there are two of us. There is the "self" that we show others and then there is the self that we are when we're alone. Of course, in truth there is only one of us but sometimes we feel that who we are needs to be improved upon or changed depending on who we are with.

Pick a time when you weren't your *true* self and rewrite the story. How would it have been different if you had been yourself?

_____

_____

_____

_____

_____

_____

_____

_____

_____

_____

_____

I?I?I?I?I?I?I?I?I?I?I?I?I?I?I?

If someone said,
"Write a sentence about your life,"
I'd write, "I want to go outside and play."

Jenna Elfman

★ What would you write if someone told you to write a sentence about *your* life?

66 ————————————————

————————————————————————————

————————————————————————————

————————————————————————————— 99

You can't change the music
of your soul.

Katharine Hepburn

★ Do you agree with this quote?   ☐ Yes   ☐ No

★ If you were to describe the music of your soul, what would it sound like?

_____

_____

_____

_____

★ What category would it fit into?

☐ Pop   ☐ Blues

☐ Rock 'n' Roll   ☐ Classical

☐ Hip-hop   ☐ County

☐ Soul   ☐ Other

☐ R&B   _____

★ List the people who love you
for who you really are:

1._____

2._____

3._____

4._____

5._____

6._____

7._____

8._____

9._____

10._____

Being Yourself

_____

_____

_____

_____

_____

_____

_____

_____

_____

_____

_____

_____

_____

_____

_____

_____

_____

_____

_____

_____

Being
Yourself

Being Yourself

_____

_____

_____

_____

_____

_____

_____

_____

_____

_____

_____

_____

_____

_____

_____

_____

_____

_____

_____

_____

Being Yourself

Being Yourself

_____

_____

_____

_____

_____

_____

_____

_____

_____

_____

_____

_____

_____

_____

_____

_____

_____

_____

_____

_____

two

Being Your Own Best Friend

Friendship with oneself is all-important

because without it one cannot be friends

with anyone else in the world.

Eleanor Roosevelt

Being Your Own Best Friend

Although "being your own best friend" can sound like a cliché, it is an important one. Important because we treat ourselves like crap most of the time. We say negative things to ourselves and about ourselves. We put other people's needs before our own and, on the rare occasions where we don't, we accuse ourselves of being selfish. We call ourselves fat, ugly, stupid, pathetic and a loser all in one day. We are our own worst enemy and most of the time we don't even realize it. If someone else were to talk to us the way we talked to ourselves, we would be outraged. We would yell and scream and refuse to ever speak to them again.

Please believe me when I tell you that every effort you make to change this will be the most important and worthwhile effort you ever make. Over the course of one day, if you remember *one* time to say something nice to yourself it will dramatically change you. If you remember *one* time to do something nice for yourself, it will affect how you feel for the rest of the day. Each time you remember to "be your own best friend," the happiness you feel will be noticeable not only by you, but by those around you.

As you think about and answer these questions, begin to think kindly towards yourself. When you make a list of nurturing things you can do for yourself, commit to beginning immediately. Remember that this is something you have to work at every day. It is certainly worth it, though. I honestly believe that being yourself and being a friend to yourself is the most important thing you will ever do for your happiness. By loving yourself and being kind to yourself you honor your soul. I hope that you will begin right now being gentler with yourself. I hope that these questions and quotes will help you along the way.

Still Standing

I vow,
here and now,
to never act like a ditz,
or be perceived as one.
To never try to be anyone besides myself.
To never attempt to hide my own beauty,
or make my face prettier.
I won't be conceited or hollow or shameless,
I won't tell myself I'm better than anyone,
because I'm not.
I'll never succumb to the pressures of adolescence,
or be forced into anything.
I will never let anyone tell me my dreams are impossible
or unreal or egotistical.
I don't have to hear what I don't want to.
I won't strive for popularity,
or follow in anyone else's footsteps.
I will never use my body as a weapon,
or be closed minded about anything.
If I let new experiences in,
I can accept and try to understand.
I won't be fake,
or try and lightly talk my way out of aggravating situations.
I can take it. I am strong.
I am important. I am me.
That is why I'm still standing.

Sara Beth Cowan

Being Your Own Best Friend

★ Name ten things you like about yourself (yes, again):

1. _____
2. _____
3. _____
4. _____
5. _____
6. _____
7. _____
8. _____
9. _____
10. _____

★ What does it mean to be your own best friend?

_____

_____

_____

_____

_____

★ Give one example of a time when you were your own best friend:

_____

_____

_____

_____

_____

_____

_____

★ List ten things you judge yourself for:

1. _____

2. _____

3. _____

4. _____

5. _____

6. _____

7. _____

8. _____

9. _____

10. _____

Do you put yourself down around others? ☐ Yes ☐ No

Are you harder on yourself than on other people? ☐ Yes ☐ No

★ Do you ever feel *inferior* because of:

* The way you look?
* The way you act?
* What you believe in?
* Your background?
* Your parents' finances?

* The color of your skin?
* The clothes you wear?
* Your social status?
* Your grades?
* Your age?

★ Do you ever feel *superior* because of:

* The way you look?
* The way you act?
* What you believe in?
* Your background?
* Your parents' finances?

* The color of your skin?
* The clothes you wear?
* Your social status?
* Your grades?
* Your age?

★ Write about a time you were true to yourself even though you knew it wasn't the popular thing to do:

_____

_____

_____

_____

_____

_____

★ Describe a time when you felt alone and only had yourself to rely on:

_____

_____

_____

_____

★ What are some improvements you can make so that you can be a better friend to yourself?

_____

_____

_____

_____

_____

★ Do you treat yourself better or worse than you treat your friends? Give an example:

_____

_____

_____

_____

_____

_____

_____

_____

★ If you treated your friend as you did yourself, would you be considered a good friend? Why?

_____

_____

_____

_____

_____

_____

_____

_____

★ Name ten things you want to start doing now to treat your-self better:

1. _____

2. _____

3. _____

4. _____

5. _____

6. _____

7. _____

8. _____

9. _____

10. _____

★ Write about how your life will be different once you start doing these ten things:

_____

_____

_____

_____

_____

_____

★ Make a list of ten things you've done that you feel good about:

1. _____

2. _____

3. _____

4. _____

5. _____

6. _____

7. _____

8. _____

9. _____

10. _____

★ How did you feel when you accomplished these things?

_____

_____

_____

_____

_____

_____

Dear Friend

Write a letter to your best friend to tell her how she has encouraged you to be a better friend to yourself:

Dear _____,

_____

_____

_____

_____

_____

_____

_____

_____

_____

_____

_____

_____

_____

_____

_____

_____

_____

Best Friend's Pages

★ In what ways do I treat myself well?

_____

_____

_____

_____

_____

_____

_____

★ In what ways do I not treat myself well?

_____

_____

_____

_____

_____

_____

_____

★ In what ways do I take care of myself:

✓ Physically? _____

_____

_____

_____

✓ Emotionally? _____

_____

_____

_____

✓ Intellectually? _____

_____

_____

_____

✓ Spiritually? _____

_____

_____

_____

★ In what ways could I improve the way I take care of myself:

✓ Physically? _____

_____

_____

_____

✓ Emotionally? _____

_____

_____

_____

✓ Intellectually? _____

_____

_____

_____

✓ Spiritually? _____

_____

_____

_____

★ How do I treat myself in comparison to the way I treat my friends? Please give examples:

Better? _____

_____

_____

_____

_____

_____

_____

?¿?¿?¿?¿?¿?¿?¿?¿?¿?¿?¿?¿

Worse? _____

_____

_____

_____

_____

_____

_____

★ As my best friend, please tell me what I can do to be a better friend to myself:

_____

_____

_____

_____

_____

_____

_____

_____

_____

★ Will you support and encourage me to do those things?

_____

_____

_____

_____

_____

_____

The following pages are so important. Take your time with them and use them as a loving reminder to be as kind to yourself as you would want to be to your dearest friend.

These pages can also be done with your best friend. They make great topics for discussion, as well.

> When you feel good about yourself,
> others will feel good
> about you, too.
>
> Jake Steinfeld

★ Do you think this is true?   ☐ Yes   ☐ No

★ List ten good reasons to be a friend to yourself:

1. _____

2. _____

3. _____

4. _____

5. _____

6. _____

7. _____

8. _____

9. _____

10. _____

Happiness is a gift. But it cannot be given to you by other people; you give it to yourself.

Jacqueline Kehoe

★ Do you accept responsibility
  for your own happiness?   ☐ Yes   ☐ No

★ In what ways do you give yourself happiness?

_____

_____

_____

_____

_____

_____

_____

_____

★ List ways and things you can do to "be your own best friend":

1. _____
2. _____
3. _____
4. _____
5. _____
6. _____
7. _____
8. _____
9. _____
10. _____

My Greatest Friend

I am only I.
There is no one here but me.
I won't bother to deny
That what I am is what you see.

I used to let it hurt
When your words would cut me down
When your voice was cold and curt
And I was too afraid to even frown.

But now I know I'm better
Than you led me to believe.
So I'm writing you this letter
To tell you what you didn't perceive.

I am invincible.
I get my strength from me.
My grace is indestructible
And my heart can clearly see.

I am a shining star
With beauty from inside.
I have wings to fly me far
And my soul is true and tried.

I am the gold that's bright
I'll never fade away.
Life is fail or fight
And I am here to stay.

I'll no longer listen to your lies.
My heart is on the mend.
I know that I am only I
And I am my closest friend.

Megan Kimm Snook

Being Your Own Best Friend

Being Your Own
Best Friend

_____

_____

_____

_____

_____

_____

_____

_____

_____

_____

_____

_____

_____

_____

_____

_____

_____

_____

_____

_____

_____

Being Your Own Best Friend

Being Your Own Best Friend

_____

_____

_____

_____

_____

_____

_____

_____

_____

_____

_____

_____

_____

_____

_____

_____

_____

_____

_____

_____

_____

Being Your Own Best Friend

Being Your Own Best Friend

_____

_____

_____

_____

_____

_____

_____

_____

_____

_____

_____

_____

_____

_____

_____

_____

_____

_____

_____

_____

three

What Is Friendship?

Friendship is a dance of give-and-take

between people who have chosen

to care for one another.

Kimberly Kirberger

What Is Friendship?

The real friend is he or she who can share
all our sorrow and double our joys.

B.C. Forbes

**Every friendship is unique and everyone's definition
of friendship is different.** There are, however, words that
come up over and over again when one talks about friendship. On our Web site we posted the question: Use three
words to describe what friendship is to you. The most common word was *trust*.

It is interesting how important trust is in friendship. I think
in order to open up to another person and show your real
self, you have to trust them. If you are going to ask their opinion, go along with their plans and tell them your secrets, you
have to trust them. Before our hearts feel safe, we need to
know that the other person will not hurt us.

In this chapter you will not only be asked to describe what
friendship means to you, but also to describe the most

important trait you look for in a friend. It is important to look closely at your thoughts and feelings on this one because they will affect how you choose friends in the future and will also affect the kind of friend you choose to be.

A True Friend

As I gazed out my window,
Thoughts swarmed through my head.
Questions unanswered left me thinking,
Long after I went to bed.

I woke up the next morning,
My thoughts still a mystery.
When a question took hold,
What could a true friend be?

I sat down to ponder,
The meaning of friend.
Are they someone you trust?
Are there rules that they bend?

Many answers came to me,
As I sat there and thought.
A friend is a special person,
That cannot be bought.

A friend is someone loving,
Someone who listens and shares.
A friend is someone trusting,
Someone who truly cares.

A true friend is real.
When you look in their eyes.
When you see into their soul,
And not find any lies.

Pieces fall into place,
And suddenly things aren't so blue.
As I begin to realize,
That my true friend is you.

My thoughts run smoothly now,
As my answer becomes clear.
My emotions are all over the place,
Down my cheek trails a tear.

You are my special friend,
One who has helped me pull through.
Now I hope I can be,
That same special friend to you.

Candace Schoonhoven

What Is Friendship?

★ What does friendship mean to you?

_____

_____

_____

_____

_____

_____

_____

_____

★ Why are your friends your friends?

_____

_____

_____

_____

_____

_____

_____

★ Why is friendship important to you?

_____

_____

_____

_____

_____

_____

_____

★ What qualities do you look for in a friend?

1. _____

2. _____

3. _____

4. _____

5. _____

6. _____

7. _____

8. _____

9. _____

10. _____

★ In what ways are your friends similar to you? In what ways are they different?

Similar? _____

_____

_____

_____

Different? _____

_____

_____

_____

★ Has your definition of friendship changed over the past few years? In what ways?

_____

_____

_____

_____

_____

_____

_____

A. K. A. Friend

One to confide in,
There 'til the end,
Shares my deep secrets,
A.K.A. friend.

Lifts up my spirits,
My heart she can mend,
Wipes away teardrops,
A.K.A. friend.

She smiles when I'm happy,
But a shoulder she'll lend,
Whenever I'm lonely
A.K.A. friend.

Helps fight my battles,
She's here to defend,
If she's here I'll be safe,
A.K.A. friend.

Jessica Cox

Dear Friend

Write a note to your friend and tell her or him what your friendship means to you:

Dear _____,

_____

_____

_____

_____

_____

_____

_____

_____

_____

_____

_____

_____

_____

_____

_____

Best Friend's Pages

★ What do you think is the strongest part of our friendship?

_____

_____

_____

_____

_____

★ List the qualities that you look for in a friend:

1. _____

2. _____

3. _____

4. _____

5. _____

6. _____

7. _____

8. _____

9. _____

10. _____

★ Describe our friendship:

_____

_____

_____

_____

_____

_____

_____

_____

★ What do you like best about our friendship?

_____

_____

_____

_____

_____

_____

_____

The Oath of a True Friend

When you need a hand to hold
I will extend mine.
When it's dark, and you are lost
I will be your light.
When you feel that you are all alone
I will always be near.
When you are crying
I will dry your tears.
When you are afraid
I will calm your fears.
When you need an escape
I will give you a place to hide.
When you feel there is no one else,
I will stick by your side.
When you need help
All you have to do is call my name.
And when you change,
I will love you just the same.

Alejandra Capdevila

Take your time on these next few pages. On the blank pages at the end of this chapter write your own quotes and poetry. Be aware of how friendships and how you define them change from day to day. Also be aware of the things about friendships that never change.

The true way and the sure way to friendship is through humility—being open to each other, accepting each other just as we are.

Mother Teresa

★ What does it mean to be humble?

_____

_____

_____

_____

_____

★ Do you ever have trouble accepting people "as they are"? Give examples:

_____

_____

_____

_____

_____

A circle is round, it has no end
That's how long I want
to be your friend!

Anonymous

★ Do you have a friend you feel this way about?

□ Yes   □ No

★ Write her or him a letter or write a poem about your friendship:

_____

_____

_____

_____

_____

_____

_____

_____

_____

True friends are the ones who really
know you but love you anyway.

Edna Buchanan

When I read this quote I think about the people I have known the longest. I think about the friends I have had for many years who have seen me through all kinds of stages. The friends who love me in spite of all the mistakes I have made are the friends who help me to love and accept myself.

★ Who does this quote make you think of and why?

66 _____

_____

_____

_____

_____

_____

_____

_____

_____

_____ 99

Happiness is achieved only by
making others happy.

Stuart Cloete

★ Do you agree with this statement? ☐ Yes ☐ No

★ Write about a time when you helped someone else and it made you happy:

I remember when _____

_____

_____

_____

_____

_____

_____

_____

_____

_____

_____

Our opinion of people depends less upon what we see in them than upon what they make us see in ourselves.

Sara Grand

★ Do you agree with this statement?   ☐ Yes   ☐ No

★ What have your friends helped you to see in yourself?

_____

_____

_____

_____

_____

_____

_____

_____

_____

_____

The only way to have a
friend is to be one.

Ralph Waldo Emerson

★ What does he mean?

66 _____

_____

_____

_____

_____

_____ 99

★ Have you ever made a friend simply because they liked you
first? Describe when this happened:

_____

_____

_____

_____

_____

_____

It is not what you give your friend,
but what you are willing to give him that
determines the quality of friendship.

Mary Dixon Thayer

★ Do you agree with this quote?   ☐ Yes   ☐ No

★ What are you willing to give to your closest friends?

_____

_____

_____

_____

_____

_____

_____

_____

_____

_____

_____

I think best friends are the ones who
have been through what you've been through.
They understand where you're coming
from and where you're going.

Shannon Miller

★ Do you think that your best friends are the ones who have
been through the same things you have? Why or why not?

_____

_____

_____

_____

_____

★ Do you think it is necessary that your friends have had the
same experiences? Why or why not?

_____

_____

_____

_____

_____

A friend is someone you can be alone with and have nothing to do and not be able to think of anything to say and be comfortable in the silence.

Sheryl Condie

★ Are you comfortable with silence? ☐ Yes ☐ No

★ Are you able to just
   "be" with your friends? ☐ Yes ☐ No

★ Remember a time when you were "comfortable in the silence" with one of your friends:

_____

_____

_____

_____

_____

_____

_____

What's crucial is the sincere wish to see others become happy. And it is something we should make some effort toward each day.

Daisaku Ikeda

★ Make a list of things you *wish* for your friends. Put the name of the friend next to the wish you have for him or her:

Name　　　　　　Wish

1. _____　_____

2. _____　_____

3. _____　_____

4. _____　_____

5. _____　_____

6. _____　_____

7. _____　_____

8. _____　_____

9. _____　_____

10. _____　_____

11. _____　_____

Name   Wish

12. _____   _____

13. _____   _____

14. _____   _____

15. _____   _____

16. _____   _____

17. _____   _____

18. _____   _____

19. _____   _____

20. _____   _____

21. _____   _____

What Is Friendship?

What Is Friendship?

_____

_____

_____

_____

_____

_____

_____

_____

_____

_____

_____

_____

_____

_____

_____

_____

_____

_____

What Is Friendship?

What Is Friendship?

_____

_____

_____

_____

_____

_____

_____

_____

_____

_____

_____

_____

_____

_____

_____

_____

_____

_____

_____

What Is Friendship?

What Is Friendship?

_____

_____

_____

_____

_____

_____

_____

_____

_____

_____

_____

_____

_____

_____

_____

_____

_____

_____

_____

_____

_____

_____

four

Challenges in Friendship

Until I have had a fight with a friend or

until they have seen me at my worst,

I can't completely trust that our friendship

is one that will have depth and last.

Kimberly Kirberger

Challenges in Friendship

Life's challenges are not supposed to paralyze you; they're supposed to help you discover who you are.

Bernice Johnson Reagon

Challenges are what make us grow and become stronger and better human beings. Without challenges in friendship, we wouldn't examine ourselves and we wouldn't even learn how to be a true friend to those we love.

When we face a difficult situation with a friend, like a fight, that is when we learn about ourselves. We experience our boundaries and the way we deal with hurt, as well as seeing how our friend reacts under the same pressures.

I don't seek out disagreements with my friends and I'd rather eat brussel sprouts than have an argument, *but* I do, in most cases, feel a deeper trust once I've survived a fight or argument and we both were able to work through it.

Remember not to avoid or shy away from necessary confrontations or dealing head-on with a challenge. Just remember: Though not fun, challenges make you a better and stronger person.

Challenges in Friendship

★ What are the most challenging aspects of friendship?

_____

_____

_____

_____

★ What was the greatest challenge you have faced in a friendship so far?

_____

_____

_____

_____

★ Make a list of things you would consider damaging to a friendship:

1. _____

2. _____

3. _____

4. _____

5. _____

Dear Friend

Write a note to your best friend about the challenges you have faced together and how you made it through:

Dear _____,

_____

_____

_____

_____

_____

_____

_____

_____

_____

_____

_____

_____

_____

_____

_____

_____

Best Friend's Pages

★ What are some challenges our friendship has endured?

_____

_____

_____

_____

★ Have I ever made choices that were hard for you to accept?
What were they?

_____

_____

_____

★ What do you think we fight about or disagree on the most?

_____

_____

_____

★ What values do we both strongly stand by?

_____

_____

_____

_____

_____

_____

_____

★ What do you think has been the most difficult challenge we have had to overcome in our friendship?

_____

_____

_____

_____

_____

_____

_____

_____

Think about the things in your life that have caused you to grow as a person. For me, most of those memories are of times when I was forced to change because my behavior or my poor judgment was causing me pain. As much as we all hate and work hard to avoid confrontations, fights or even loss, it is from those very things that we become better people.

Over the next few pages, you will have the opportunity to take a look at the challenges you have overcome in your friendships and how those challenges have affected the person you are today.

A good friend isn't surprised by
your mistakes. She expects them. Somewhere,
fairly early in the relationship, a good friend will
find out the truth about you. She'll witness your
weaknesses firsthand. And it's at this point
that your friend, if she's really a good friend,
will decide to stick by you anyway.

Caron Loveless

★ Who does this quote make you think of?

_____

_____

_____

_____

_____

_____

_____

★ Have you told them thanks? ☐ Yes ☐ No

Can miles truly separate us from friends?
If we want to be with someone we love,
aren't we already there?

Richard Bach

★ What do you think about this quote?

66 _____

_____

_____

_____

_____ 99

★ Do you have any friends who live far away? If so, how do
you feel about them?

_____

_____

_____

_____

_____

If you love someone . . . you will always
believe in him, always expect the best of him,
and always stand your ground in defending him.

1 Corinthians 13:7

Many times we are challenged when it comes to doing the three things listed above. For instance: You walk out of class and see your boyfriend talking to your friend. She's laughing extra loud and touching his arm. It looks like she is *flirting* big time. Do you automatically assume the worst?

Describe a situation when you . . .

★ Didn't believe in your friend:

_____

_____

_____

_____

★ Didn't expect the best of her or him:

_____

_____

_____

_____

★ Didn't defend him or her:

_____

_____

_____

★ Did believe in your friend:

_____

_____

_____

_____

★ Did expect the best of her or him:

_____

_____

_____

_____

★ Did defend him or her:

_____

_____

_____

A friend loveth at all times.

Proverbs 17:17

★ What are some of the challenges you face in "loving your friends" at all times?

_____

_____

_____

_____

_____

_____

_____

_____

_____

_____

_____

_____

One who looks for a friend without faults will have none.

Hasidic Saying

★ Do you allow your friends their faults? ☐ Yes ☐ No
★ Do you forgive yourself
   for your shortcomings? ☐ Yes ☐ No

It can be hard to break the friendship code of secrecy, and make your friend mad at you, but you must do what you feel in your heart is right.

Amanda Ford

★ Have you ever broken a promise
   to keep something a secret?   ☐ Yes ☐ No

★ Has a friend ever told someone else something about you that they were supposed to keep secret, but they thought it was best for you? Describe it.

_____

_____

_____

_____

_____

_____

_____

★ Have you ever told someone a friend's secret, but you did it for their own safety or well-being? What happened?

_____

_____

_____

_____

_____

_____

_____

There's a difference between listening and hearing; one hears with their ears, and one listens with their heart.

Hayley Gibson

♡ ♡ ♡ ♡ ♡ ♡ ♡ ♡ ♡ ♡ ♡ ♡ ♡ ♡

★ In what ways are you a good listener?

_____

_____

_____

_____

_____

★ Which of your friends do you feel most "heard" by? What is it they do to make you feel they are really listening?

_____

_____

_____

_____

_____

_____

Challenges in Friendship

Challenges in Friendship

_____

_____

_____

_____

_____

_____

_____

_____

_____

_____

_____

_____

_____

_____

_____

_____

_____

_____

_____

_____

Challenges in Friendship

Challenges in Friendship

_____

_____

_____

_____

_____

_____

_____

_____

_____

_____

_____

_____

_____

_____

_____

_____

_____

_____

_____

_____

_____

Challenges in Friendship

Challenges in Friendship

_____

_____

_____

_____

_____

_____

_____

_____

_____

_____

_____

_____

_____

_____

_____

_____

_____

_____

_____

_____

five

Making Friends

You can make more friends in two months

by becoming interested in other people

than you can in two years by trying to get

other people interested in you.

Dale Carnegie

Making Friends

How sad to think of what might have been—
So, go! Take a chance and make a friend!

Rocky Henriques

Making friends is one of the most important things you will ever do.

Many of us just sort of fall into friendships, which can be fine. We meet people through our school, our groups, or our jobs and they become our friends. What we need to remember is to not take our friends for granted, and that true friendship only occurs with an effort or, I should say, a *continued* effort. Friendship is that good feeling you get when you have come through for someone, fulfilled a need, listened and listened some more. It is also important that as a friend you are open and able to receive the love and support your friend has to offer you.

Friendship, like anything in life, requires energy and care. But there are few things that will give you back as much joy and happiness as a good friendship does.

Rose

A splendid rose stood,
all alone.
Surrounded by a wall
of stone.
Around the wall were
roses, too.
Still neither knew the
other grew.
So often we, like flowers
dwell
Too deep within our
human shell.
And pass through life
not understood.
Nor making all the friends
We should.

Christi Bergschneider
Teen.com

Making Friends

★ What qualities do you look for in a friend?

1. _____
2. _____
3. _____
4. _____
5. _____
6. _____
7. _____
8. _____
9. _____
10. _____

★ What qualities do you avoid?

1. _____
2. _____
3. _____
4. _____
5. _____

6. _____

7. _____

8. _____

9. _____

10. _____

★ Is it easy or difficult for you to make new friends?

□ *Easy*   □ *Difficult*

★ What do you feel is the most frightening part of making new friends?

_____

_____

_____

★ Who was the first friend you ever made?

_____

★ How did it happen?

_____

_____

_____

★ Where and when did you make most of your current and closest friends?

_____

_____

_____

_____

★ Have you ever initially passed judgment on someone who later became a friend? Describe how you realized that you were wrong about him or her:

_____

_____

_____

_____

_____

_____

★ Are you open-minded about who you make friends with or do you stick with a particular group?

_____

_____

_____

_____

★ Have you ever had to move to a new town or change schools?

☐ *Yes*   ☐ *No*

★ If so, how did you make new friends?

_____

_____

_____

_____

★ When was the last time you made a new friend?

_____

*W*rite about a time when you took a chance on someone and it turned out great:

_____

_____

_____

_____

_____

_____

_____

Dear Friend

Write a story for your best friend about how the two of you met and became friends:

Dear _____,

_____

_____

_____

_____

_____

_____

_____

_____

_____

_____

_____

_____

_____

_____

_____

_____

Best Friend's Pages

★ Honestly, what did you think about me upon our first meeting?

_____

_____

_____

_____

_____

_____

★ When did you realize you wanted to be my friend?

_____

_____

_____

_____

★ Do you remember our first conversation? What was it about?

_____

_____

_____

_____

★ Describe a time when you were grateful that we became friends:

_____

_____

_____

_____

_____

★ When do you feel our friendship really blossomed?

_____

_____

_____

_____

_____

★ When was the first time you opened up to me?

_____

_____

_____

_____

_____

★ When was the first time I opened up to you?

_____

_____

_____

_____

_____

★ Do you think I have changed since we first became friends?
In what ways?

_____

_____

_____

_____

_____

★ Are we open to meeting new people or do we prefer to
stick with the friends we have?

_____

_____

_____

_____

_____

Clouded Memory

If only for a coincidence in our lives
I found you, my friend.
Introducing ourselves with curious glances
Although somehow always knowing
I'd passed you this way before.
We were strangers journeying
Along foreign streets
But security was found
When I discovered you
Like a priceless treasure
Uncovered by fortune
In our dust along that road.
Now as I turn again and look behind me
I see a cloud of memories,
Of journeys along foreign streets
When our paths crossed,
And I stumbled,
And found a friend.

Anne G. Fegely

When making new friends, it is important to think about things like:

- What is important to you in friendship?
- What kinds of things do you expect from your friends, and are you prepared to give them the same things in return?
- Is it necessary that your friends have the same values as you?
- Is it necessary that your friends share the same interests as you?

I am sure there are other questions that are important to think about when it comes to making new friends, but this is a good place to start. The more aware you are of these things now, the better chance you have of making friendships that will last and be positive additions to your life.

But along the way you make friends.
Good friends. And you help each other realize
that all the things you want to be—
you already are.

Gretchen
Dawson's Creek

★ What do you think about this quote?

66 _____

_____

_____

_____

_____ 99

★ Make a list of some qualities that your friends have helped you to realize you have:

1. _____

2. _____

3. _____

4. _____

5. _____

6. _____

7. _____

8. _____

9. _____

10. _____

11. _____

12. _____

*You only meet your once-in-a-lifetime friend
... once in a lifetime.*

Little Rascals

★ Have you met your once-in-a-lifetime friend? Describe him or her:

_____

_____

_____

_____

_____

_____

_____

_____

_____

_____

_____

_____

_____

So I started hanging out with Rayanne Graff. Just for fun. Just cause it seemed like if I didn't, I would die or something.

Angela

My So-Called Life

★ Do you have any friends who you feel this way about? Describe why you feel this way about them:

?

My means of empowerment has always been to search out wonderful friends, people who believe in me, who help me believe in myself.

Sandy Warshaw

★ Can your choice of friends make a difference in how the world perceives you and treats you?

☐ Yes   ☐ No

★ In what ways?

_____

_____

_____

_____

_____

_____

_____

_____

Be true with yourself and others and
the friends that you make
will be the best ones.

Nico Aguayo

★ What does this quote mean to you?

_____

_____

_____

_____

_____

_____

_____

_____

_____

_____

_____

_____

_____

Always having a positive attitude when
meeting someone new can lead
to great friendships.

Christine Kalinowski

★ Do you agree with this quote? Why or why not?

66 _____

_____

_____

_____ 99

★ How has a positive attitude helped you in making new friends?

_____

_____

_____

_____

_____

_____

Nothing in life is to be feared.
It is only to be understood.

Marie Curie

We often shy away from getting too close to people because we are afraid we'll get hurt.

★ Do you think if you understood yourself and your life more you would be less afraid to open up to others? In what ways would understanding yourself better help you in your relationships?

_____

_____

_____

_____

_____

_____

_____

_____

_____

_____

Have you ever had your day suddenly
turn sunshiny because of a cheerful word?
You can make today the same for somebody.
It is only a question of a little imagination,
a little time and trouble.

Maltbie D. Babcock

★ Make a promise to yourself that you will make someone happy with an act of kindness. Write about what you plan to do:

_____

_____

_____

_____

★ Afterwards, write about how your act of kindness was received:

_____

_____

_____

_____

Making Friends

_____

_____

_____

_____

_____

_____

_____

_____

_____

_____

_____

_____

_____

_____

_____

_____

_____

_____

_____

_____

Making Friends

Making Friends

Making Friends

Making Friends

_____

_____

_____

_____

_____

_____

_____

_____

_____

_____

_____

_____

_____

_____

_____

_____

_____

_____

_____

_____

_____

_____

_____

_____

_____

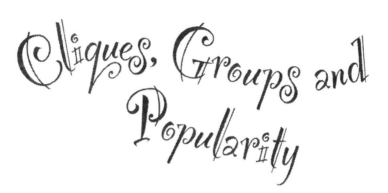

six

Cliques, Groups and Popularity

You don't get harmony when

everybody sings the

same note.

Doug Floyd

Cliques, Groups and Popularity

Great individuals are not
only popular themselves, but they give
popularity to whatever
they touch.

Fournier

For some people, the mere mention of the words "cliques," "groups" or "popularity" can produce panic and uncomfortable feelings. I, for one, suffered many times over things like popularity and whether or not I fit in with a certain group or clique. I don't know of anyone who has escaped being devastated at one time or another by these things. It is because of the times we have been hurt that we tend to have a negative association with cliques and the word "popularity" but, if we think about it, these things also provide comfort and a sense of belonging. For instance, the cliques that we become a part of can have many positive aspects to them as

151

well. They are our home base and give us the security of always having a group of friends to turn to.

Popularity may be a little harder to see in a positive light, especially if we feel we lack it. The thing about popularity is that it isn't objective and, in many ways, it is just an illusion that some enjoy and others suffer from. In order to be able to hear these words without cringing, just remember that what is important is having some good friends and learning to be a friend to yourself. It may sound like too simple a solution, but it really is what will matter in the end.

Cliques, Groups and Popularity

★ Are you part of a group or clique?   ☐ Yes   ☐ No

★ Are there words that others use to describe your group like preps, skaters, etc.?

_____

_____

_____

_____

_____

_____

_____

★ Does your group exclude others? Who?

_____

_____

_____

_____

_____

_____

★ Have you ever made fun of or excluded someone from your group because of:

☛ The group they were in?   ☛ How they looked?

☛ The way they dressed?   ☛ Their weight?

☛ The color of their skin?   ☛ Other reasons?

☛ Their financial standing?

★ How did that make you feel?

_____

_____

_____

_____

★ Has anyone ever made fun of or excluded you because of:

☛ The group they were in?   ☛ How they looked?

☛ The way they dressed?   ☛ Their weight?

☛ The color of their skin?   ☛ Other reasons?

☛ Their financial standing?

★ How did that make you feel?

_____

_____

_____

_____

★ Describe a time when you felt left out by yours or any clique and how it made you feel:

_____

_____

_____

_____

_____

★ Write about a time that you felt ashamed to be associated with your clique. Why did you feel this way and what did you do about it?

_____

_____

_____

_____

_____

★ Has there ever been anything you've done for popularity that you really regretted later on?

_____

_____

_____

_____

★ Have you ever lied to improve your social status? Tell about it:

_____

_____

_____

_____

_____

★ What do people think about the group you're in?

_____

_____

_____

_____

_____

★ Why do you believe they think this way?

_____

_____

_____

_____

_____

★ What are the positive things you get from being in a group?

Positive _____

_____

_____

_____

_____

★ What are the negative things about being in a group?

Negative _____

_____

_____

_____

_____

★ Do you think popularity is important? Why or why not?

_____

_____

_____

_____

_____

_____

★ What makes a person "popular"?

_____

_____

_____

_____

_____

★ Do you ever evaluate people based on their popularity? In what ways?

_____

_____

_____

_____

_____

★ Do you ever evaluate yourself based on your popularity? In what ways?

_____

_____

_____

_____

_____

★ Would you rather be popular or have a few true and genuine friends? Explain:

_____

_____

_____

_____

_____

_____

_____

★ Analyze yourself and decide why you do or do not "fit in" with the group that you do:

_____

_____

_____

_____

_____

_____

_____

★ What central bond unites your group?

_____

_____

_____

_____

_____

★ Do you feel that you had to change yourself in any way to fit into your clique?

_____

_____

_____

_____

_____

★ Have you ever felt like you didn't fit in with any particular group or clique?

_____

_____

_____

_____

_____

★ In a short paragraph, describe your group like a journalist would. Be as objective as possible:

_____

_____

_____

_____

_____

★ List five reasons why you are grateful for your group of friends:

1. _____

2. _____

3. _____

4. _____

5. _____

★ Write about the best time you have had with your group of friends:

_____

_____

_____

_____

Dear Friend

Write a note to your best friend about how he or she makes you feel like you belong:

Dear _____,

_____

_____

_____

_____

_____

_____

_____

_____

_____

_____

_____

_____

_____

_____

_____

Best Friend's Pages

★ Are there things we could do to be more tolerant of others?

_____

_____

_____

_____

_____

_____

_____

_____

_____

★ List five things you want us to try to change in terms of how we treat others:

1. _____

2. _____

3. _____

4. _____

5. _____

★ Have I ever excluded you?   ☐ Yes   ☐ No

★ How did you feel?

_____

_____

_____

_____

★ Have you ever excluded me?   ☐ Yes   ☐ No

★ How did you feel?

_____

_____

_____

_____

★ Have I ever left you out around a certain group of people?

☐ Yes   ☐ No

★ If so, how did that feel?

_____

_____

_____

_____

Part of growing up is forming a self—knowing who you are and what you need and want from life and from your friends. Groups or cliques serve a purpose in that we try to find people similar to us who share our likes and dislikes and our values. On these next pages, think about what you get from your group, what things brought you together and, if you had a choice today, whether you would choose the same friends or not.

I bet people can actually die of embarrassment.
I bet it's been medically proven.

Angela
My So-Called Life

★ Have you ever felt like you would die from embarrassment?

☐ Yes   ☐ No

★ What happened?

_____

_____

_____

_____

_____

_____

_____

_____

_____

_____

When you make popularity your main goal,
you constantly change your personality
to fit those around you.

Amanda Ford

★ Have you ever changed who you were because you thought
it would make you more popular? Describe what happened:

_____

_____

_____

_____

_____

_____

_____

_____

_____

_____

_____

_____

Tables Turned

She thinks
"Here I come, the Queen of them all
I'm sweet and I'm pretty"
as she strides down the hall.

She carelessly talks
and speaks mindless chatter
she wanders around
continuously flattered.

She does not acknowledge
the ones who don't speak
insignificant to her
she knows they are weak.

But one day she will need them
and their incredible smarts,
she'll need their advice
that will come from their hearts.

One day she will fall
from the clouds up above
and "friends" will forget
the girl who was loved.

The ones who will help her
the ones who will care
are the ones she walked past
with her nose in the air.

They know what it's like
to be ignored by them all
the ones who buzz by
when they walk down the hall.

They promised themselves
they would never be cruel
they acknowledge everyone
who goes to this school.

So always remember
when your popularity ends
the ones who will empathize
are the ones with no friends.

If they walk kind of funny
or their hair is a mess
they never looked twice
at the way that you dress.

Even though they are different
and not at all like you,
it's important to remember
that they're human, too.

Leah Houston

It is pointless to be caught up in outward appearances. If we are sincere, people will understand our intentions, and our positive qualities will radiate.

Daisaku Ikeda

★ Do you believe this quote?   ☐ Yes   ☐ No

★ Can you give an example of a time when you were impressed or moved by someone's intentions and positive "inner" qualities?

_____

_____

_____

_____

_____

_____

_____

_____

_____

_____

Everything in life isn't about winning.
You have to find joy in the process.
You have to love what you do.

Joey
Dawson's Creek

★ Are you competitive with your friends? ☐ Yes ☐ No

★ In what ways?

_____

_____

_____

_____

★ Does competition make you uncomfortable? Why or why not?

_____

_____

_____

_____

★ Do you think it's possible to forgive while still being clear about how you expect to be treated?

☐ Yes ☐ No

Cliques, Groups and Popularity

Cliques, Groups and Popularity

Cliques, Groups and Popularity

_____

_____

_____

_____

_____

_____

_____

_____

_____

_____

_____

_____

_____

_____

_____

_____

_____

_____

_____

_____

_____

Cliques, Groups and Popularity

Cliques, Groups and Popularity

_____

_____

_____

_____

_____

_____

_____

_____

_____

_____

_____

_____

_____

_____

_____

_____

_____

_____

_____

_____

_____

seven

Friends and Lovers

The line between love and friendship

can be so thin that it is often invisible to the eye.

But if you ask your heart, odds are

you'll get the right answer.

Kimberly Kirberger

Friends and Lovers

Love is a friendship caught on fire.

Northern Exposure

This is a tricky situation because the feelings that you have for a friend are not that far off from the feelings that you have when you are attracted to someone. Remove the physicality and they are almost exactly the same. I have been asked many times by teens, "How do I know if I like him as a friend or as a boyfriend?" Good question!!! I have two answers and I wouldn't swear by either one.

First I would say, "You know the answer in your heart." Secondly I would say, "Kiss him and you'll know." As I said, I wouldn't swear by either one, but they are better than torturing yourself by wondering so much that by the time you figure it out he is professing his love for someone else and coming to you for advice. Unfortunately, at this moment you will know for sure if you felt something more than friendship because your heart will feel like a very sharp knife is stabbing it. What I am trying to say is, whether you are the one who is confused or you are the object of someone else's confusion, talk about it. Talk about it NOW. And, if at all possible, talk about it with the actual person in question as opposed to everyone else.

We also address in this chapter the very common situation of placing our lovers above our friends. If I can be honest here, I have to say that when you fall in love with someone and you are lucky enough to have the feelings be mutual, it is a very wonderful thing. It is so wonderful that when our friends want us to hang out with them instead of going out with our boyfriend, it is a very difficult decision to make. More often than not, we put too much pressure on ourselves and on our friends to choose friendship over love. BUT with that said, we do have to remember who listened to us when we were boyfriend-less or who will be there when the relationship ends. The answer: Don't place unrealistic pressures on yourself or on your friends to always choose friendship over love. BUT do make time for your friends and make that time special by being there 100 percent.

Friends and Lovers

★ Have you ever had a friend that you fell in love with?

☐ Yes   ☐ No

★ If so, what happened and how did it turn out?

_____

_____

_____

_____

_____

_____

_____

_____

_____

★ Has a friend ever fallen in love with you?

☐ Yes   ☐ No

★ How did it turn out?

_____

_____

_____

_____

★ Have you ever had to give someone "the friend talk"? (You know the one: "Our friendship is more important. . . . I think of you as a friend. . . . ")

_____

_____

_____

_____

★ Do you think it is possible to have a purely platonic, or non-sexual, relationship with a person of the opposite sex?

☐ Yes   ☐ No

Explain your answer:

_____

_____

_____

_____

★ Do you have many friends of the opposite sex?

☐ *Yes* ☐ *No*

★ Is it at all possible that you have feelings that are a bit more than friendly for any of them?

☐ *Yes* ☐ *No*

★ Do you think there are reasons that it is better to remain friends rather than let the relationship develop into more?

_____

_____

_____

_____

★ Do you think any of your friends share a secret crush on you?

☐ *Yes* ☐ *No*

★ Do you feel the same way? ☐ *Yes* ☐ *No*

★ What would it take for it to develop into a "relationship"?

_____

_____

_____

_____

★ Have you ever ignored your friends because you wanted to only be with your boyfriend or girlfriend?

☐ Yes   ☐ No

★ Have you ever lost a friend when he or she got into a relationship? Describe what happened:

_____

_____

_____

_____

_____

_____

_____

_____

_____

_____

_____

_____

_____

Dear Friend

Write a note to your best friend to thank him or her for making your friendship a priority and for listening when you are having a love problem.

Dear _____,

_____

_____

_____

_____

_____

_____

_____

_____

_____

_____

_____

_____

_____

_____

_____

_____

_____

Best Friend's Pages

★ Do you ever feel like I spend too much time with my boyfriend or girlfriend and not enough with you?

☐ Yes   ☐ No

★ How does it feel?

_____

_____

_____

_____

_____

_____

★ What do you think is more important: friends or lovers? Explain:

_____

_____

_____

_____

★ Do you think guys and girls can be purely platonic friends?

☐ Yes   ☐ No

★ Do we have a clear understanding that we wouldn't go near each other's crushes or exes? Has this understanding ever been broken?

_____

_____

_____

_____

★ What happened?

_____

_____

_____

_____

★ What is our unspoken agreement regarding each other's exes and crushes?

_____

_____

_____

_____

★ Would you tell me if you had feelings for a friend of ours?
Why or why not?

_____

_____

_____

_____

_____

_____

_____

★ Do you think I feel more than friendship for any of our
friends? If so, tell me why.

_____

_____

_____

_____

_____

_____

_____

It is no big mystery why two friends would develop more than "friendly" feelings for one another. Nor is it a mystery why a person would befriend someone they were interested in. What I often wonder is, why does it have to be so complicated and messy? Why can't two people who are friends tell each other, "We'll check it out and see what we do best—friendship or romance" and if the answer is friendship, then just go back to being friends?

What do you think are the reasons that the "friends and lovers" question is so complicated?

My Friend

You, my friend, my old best friend,
　my life, my dream, my love.
You, my friend, who'd lift me up
　to heaven and above.
Is it possible for you, my friend,
　to take my love away?
Because, my friend, I do recall
　your words that read you'd stay.
A friend's supposed to tell the truth,
　a friend's supposed to care.
You claim to be my best friend still,
　a friend who's never there.
You may have been my friend at first,
　and my friend you'll always be.

But a friendship goes both ways, you know,
    I wonder when you'll see.

My friend, I guess if all else fails,
    that angels up above

Have taught us both a lesson:
    Best friends can't fall in love.

Because, my friend, I'll love you so
    until the day I die.

But I need your friendship for right now
    if your love is but a lie.

You see, my friend, you owe me more
    than you ever will realize.

And if you want some proof, my friend,
    you'll see it in my eyes.

Because, my friend, a tear you'll see
    but the reason for my pain,

Is that you just don't seem to care,
    and I love you just the same.

Rebecca Woolf

To be your friend was all I ever wanted;
to be your lover was all
I ever dreamed.

Valerie Lombardo

★ Is there someone you feel this way about now?

_____

_____

_____

_____

_____

_____

★ Have you *ever* felt this way about someone?

_____

_____

_____

_____

_____

_____

> So we were friends,
> then we were a couple,
> then we were friends again,
> then we were a couple . . .
> what are we now?
>
> Joey
> Dawson's Creek

★ Have you gone through anything like this? Describe what happened:

_____

_____

_____

_____

_____

_____

_____

Dawson, the last year of my life has been like this wide-awake nightmare of conflicting emotions. But no matter how bad it got, one thing kept me going. Us. Our bond, our connection, whatever you want to call it. It made me feel like I wasn't alone, like I was part of something special.

Joey

Dawson's Creek

★ Do you have a friend or lover you feel this way about? Explain your relationship:

_____

_____

_____

_____

_____

_____

_____

I'm sorry. I'm sorry for my part in it.
And I'm sorry for the pain I know it caused you.
But mostly I'm sorry because
I miss our friendship.

Pacey
Dawson's Creek

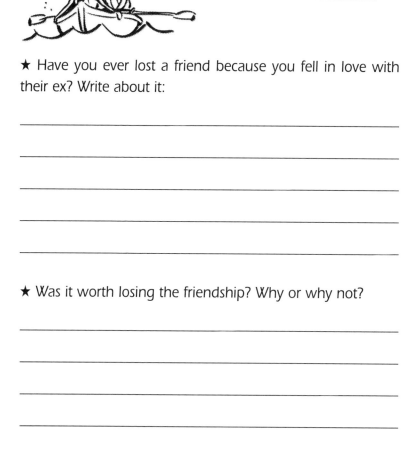

★ Have you ever lost a friend because you fell in love with their ex? Write about it:

_____

_____

_____

_____

_____

★ Was it worth losing the friendship? Why or why not?

_____

_____

_____

_____

_____

My Heart

It's been jerked and bent and twisted in knots,
It's been tangled and snarled and shamelessly
   caught.

Wounded, stabbed, hardened like a stone,
Empty, hollow, hurt and alone.

It's been squeezed and suffocated 'til I
   thought that I would choke,
Even that was bearable, until it finally broke.

Miranda Karkling

You've taught me that love can suck. That feelings can change, passion will fade, partners will come and go, but through it all, one thing remains sacred: friendship.

Dawson

Dawson's Creek

★ Are you good friends with someone you were once in a relationship with?

☐ Yes   ☐ No

★ What are your thoughts about this quote?

66

_____

_____

_____

_____

_____

_____

_____

_____

99

If you have a friend who has ditched
you for her boyfriend, let her know you are hurt.
Tell her you're happy for her, but that you
miss having her around, and you wish that she
would keep time for your friendship.

Amanda Ford

★ Have you ever gone through this with a friend?

☐ Yes   ☐ No

★ What did you do?

_____

_____

_____

_____

_____

_____

_____

_____

Friends and lovers go hand in hand
so don't be surprised if one
turns out to be the other.

Nico Aguayo

? ♡ ? ♡ ? ♡ ? ♡ ? ♡ ? ♡ ? ♡ ? ♡ ? ♡ ?

★ Do you suspect that someone you know might be hiding their feelings towards you? If so, what makes you feel this way?

_____

_____

_____

_____

_____

★ Do you have a friend who you could feel more for? Describe your feelings:

_____

_____

_____

_____

_____

Friends and Lovers

Friends and Lovers

Friends and Lovers

_____

_____

_____

_____

_____

_____

_____

_____

_____

_____

_____

_____

_____

_____

_____

_____

_____

_____

_____

Friends and Lovers

Friends and Lovers

_____

_____

_____

_____

_____

_____

_____

_____

_____

_____

_____

_____

_____

_____

_____

_____

_____

_____

_____

_____

_____

_____

_____

eight

Jealousy, Hurt and Betrayal

Just as we must have darkness

so that there can be light, we must know

pain in order to know happiness.

Kimberly Kirberger

Jealousy, Hurt and Betrayal

Before you speak, ask yourself
if what you are going to say is true, is kind,
is necessary, is helpful. If the answer is no,
maybe what you are about to say
should be left unsaid.

Bernard Meltzer

Nothing stings more than the betrayal of someone we called friend. When we accept someone as our friend we give him or her access to our heart. It is kind of like giving someone a key to your house. You do this because you trust them and you want them to be able to come visit you whenever they want. Then one day they use that key to walk into your house and steal everything. When that trust and openness is betrayed it hurts because they were able to go straight to the deepest part of us.

How much you get hurt by a friend's betrayal is dependent upon how much you trusted them—how much you loved them and opened your heart to them. When this happens to you, it is so important to remember that *it isn't about you*. This will be difficult because it *feels* like it is somehow your fault. *THIS IS NOT TRUE.* One of my favorite sayings is: "Feelings aren't facts." Just because you feel small when someone else behaves poorly doesn't mean you are. Just because you feel unlovable when someone betrays you does not mean that you are. When this happens, it is important to remind yourself of this. You will still hurt, but it helps.

Of course, the other side of this is when we betray or hurt someone we care about. We have all done it. It is very important to look closely at *why*. Did you intentionally hurt your friend or were you simply doing what you thought you had to do to defend yourself?

This chapter of questions is important because the more you understand your own behavior, the more you can understand other people's. Be honest with yourself when examining these moments and remember that we all make mistakes. The important thing is to learn from them.

At the end of this chapter we have left room for you to make a list of things you will work on. An example of this would be:

- I am going to be more aware of when I am gossiping.
- I am going to be more open-minded and accepting of people who aren't in my "group."

Don't think that you can change these things overnight because you can't. We are all human and we all do things that we wish we didn't. The idea is to become more aware of what we are doing and try to do it less. When you make a mistake, for instance spread a rumor or talk about someone behind their back, don't beat yourself up. This doesn't help. Realize what you've done, forgive yourself and move on.

When you are on the receiving end of betrayal and hurt, do all that you can to be good to yourself while going through this. Remember that emotional hurt is not unlike a physical cut. At first it bleeds and hurts a lot. It may seem at the time like it's going to hurt forever. But over time the hurt lessens and the healing begins. Before you know it you aren't even thinking about it anymore.

Remember, time heals *all* wounds, including yours!

Friends

You say that you are my friend,
Or so that is what I like to hear,
But when I needed someone to talk to,
You were never there.
I listened to your problems and helped you
as much as I could,
But now you listen to what others say,
A lot more than you should.
One day you are my friend
and the next you are talking about me.
I hope that this will make you realize
and help to make you see.
If I am wrong, I apologize
And all of my love I send,
But if I am here just for you to talk about,
Then sorry, but you are not a true friend.

Michele Booths
Teen.com

Jealousy, Hurt and Betrayal

★ What's the most hurtful thing a friend has ever done to you?

_____

_____

_____

_____

_____

_____

★ Do you feel this statement is true: The people closest to you can hurt you the most? Explain:

_____

_____

_____

_____

_____

_____

★ Have you ever been jealous of your friends? If so, in what ways?

_____

_____

_____

_____

_____

_____

_____

★ Write about a time when someone forgave you after you had hurt or betrayed him or her:

_____

_____

_____

_____

_____

_____

_____

★ Have you ever treated a friend unfairly because you were jealous of him or her? Describe it:

_____

_____

_____

_____

_____

_____

_____

★ List ten things that you would consider betrayals:

1. _____

2. _____

3. _____

4. _____

5. _____

6. _____

7. _____

8. _____

9. _____

10. _____

★ Has a friend ever been jealous of you? Describe what happened:

_____

_____

_____

_____

_____

_____

_____

_____

★ Have you ever betrayed a friend's trust? When?

_____

_____

_____

_____

_____

_____

_____

★ Do you feel that many people trust you with their secrets and problems?

Why? _____

_____

Why not? _____

_____

★ Look deep inside yourself and remember a time when you couldn't bear to forgive a friend for what they had done. What was it they did? And as you look back on it now, do you have any regrets? Is it too late to rekindle the friendship?

_____

_____

_____

_____

_____

★ Has a friend ever felt you betrayed him or her and to this day you still don't understand why? Describe what happened:

_____

_____

_____

_____

★ Have you ever hurt a friend unknowingly? If so, how?

_____

_____

_____

_____

_____

★ Have you ever regretted putting your trust in someone? When?

_____

_____

_____

_____

_____

★ Do you believe that your jealousy is a result of your insecurities? Explain:

_____

_____

_____

_____

_____

★ Do you feel that you have any traits that your friends envy or covet? Describe them:

_____

_____

_____

_____

_____

_____

_____

_____

★ What would you do if your best friend told others your biggest secret? If this has happened, describe it:

_____

_____

_____

_____

_____

_____

_____

★ What would you do if a friend told others your significant other things you had shared in private?

_____

_____

_____

_____

★ Has a friend ever lied to you about his or her plans with the intention of excluding you?

_____

_____

_____

_____

★ Has a friend ever hurt you over and over, but you still couldn't end the friendship? Why or why not?

_____

_____

_____

_____

_____

★ Write down the last three times you remember being hurt or betrayed by a friend:

1. _____

2. _____

3. _____

★ Write about the last three times you hurt or betrayed a friend:

1. _____

2. _____

3. _____

★ What kinds of things hurt your feelings?

_____

_____

_____

_____

_____

_____

_____

_____

_____

★ What are some of the things you have done that have hurt other people's feelings?

_____

_____

_____

_____

_____

_____

_____

★ Do you ever talk about your friends behind their backs?

☐ Yes   ☐ No

★ How do you feel when you hear your friends have talked about you behind your back?

_____

_____

_____

_____

_____

_____

_____

★ Do you get your feelings hurt easily?   ☐ Yes   ☐ No

★ Do you think some people get treated worse than others for no real obvious reason? Give examples:

_____

_____

_____

_____

★ What is the worst thing a friend has ever done to you?

_____

_____

_____

★ What happened?

_____

_____

_____

_____

★ Are you friends today?   ☐ Yes   ☐ No

★ Do you have two friends who don't like each other?

_____ & _____

Why? _____

_____

_____

_____

★ Do you think they might be jealous of your attention? What makes you think so?

_____

_____

_____

_____

_____

★ Do you ever feel they put you in an uncomfortable position? How does that make you feel?

_____

_____

_____

_____

_____

★ Do you get angry at your friends? ☐ Yes ☐ No

★ What kinds of things make you mad?

_____

_____

_____

_____

_____

_____

_____

★ Do you say or do mean things when you're mad? Give examples:

_____

_____

_____

_____

_____

_____

_____

_____

We don't know anything.
We're really young and we're gonna screw up a lot.
We're gonna keep changing our minds and
even sometimes our hearts. And through all that,
the only real thing we can offer
each other is forgiveness.

Joey
Dawson's Creek

★ Do you forgive easily? ☐ Yes ☐ No

★ Do your friends forgive you? ☐ Yes ☐ No

★ Do you think forgiveness is a virtue? Why?

_____

_____

_____

_____

_____

_____

Dear Friend

Is there a person in your life who you have been angry with? Do you feel like it is time to forgive and forget? If so, write a letter here telling your friend you forgive him or her and are ready to let it go and move forward. Remember: It isn't necessary that you actually show this letter to anyone. Just write it to see how you feel.

Dear _____,

_____

_____

_____

_____

_____

_____

_____

_____

_____

_____

Best Friend's Pages

★ Have I ever done anything to really hurt your feelings?
What was it?

_____

_____

_____

_____

★ In the past when we have been in fights, how did we end
up resolving them?

_____

_____

_____

_____

★ Have you ever felt that I misled you or jeopardized your
trust in me in any way?

_____

_____

_____

_____

★ Do you feel that I have ever betrayed you?

_____

_____

_____

_____

★ Is there anything that you have wanted to talk to me about, but haven't been able to for whatever reason?

_____

_____

_____

_____

★ Is there anything I do that annoys you?

_____

_____

_____

_____

★ Have you ever have a hard time believing that I am being honest?

☐ Yes   ☐ No

★ Do you trust me to not talk about you behind your back? Why or why not?

_____

_____

_____

_____

★ Do you know a secret is safe with me? What makes you feel this way?

_____

_____

_____

_____

★ Have I ever stepped over the line by flirting with your boyfriend or girlfriend or joking with you in a way that was hurtful? When?

_____

_____

_____

_____

_____

_____

One of the most common mistakes we make in our friend-ships is to assume that when a friend hurts us they did it on purpose. When we get our feelings hurt or when we feel betrayed by a friend, we immediately assume that our friend caused us this terrible pain on purpose. We think their cruelty was premeditated. This is hardly ever the case.

It is very important to understand that people, especially our friends, are flawed, just like us. I remember a friend once said to me, "If I insisted on friends who were without fault, then I would be friendless."

We make mistakes and sadly those mistakes often hurt the people that we care about. When we are hurt or we feel betrayed, it can be very helpful to take a few deep breaths before responding. Then take some time to think about what happened and what might have been going on for the other person. It is possible that they were hurt and they were just reacting to something they thought you did. It is also possible that they were going through something very difficult and just handled it poorly. And, of course, it is possible that they were just being a jerk or acting irresponsibly.

If we are honest with ourselves, we will know that we have all talked bad about someone we love. We have all told a secret that we knew our friend would rather not have others know. And we have all been mean at a time when the person we were mean to did not deserve it. The key is to first forgive ourselves for this behavior. This doesn't mean it is okay to act irresponsibly. It simply means that we accept our humanness and we forgive ourselves for making mistakes. It also means that we try hard not to make the same mistakes twice. Once we have been able to admit our shortcomings and forgive ourselves for them, then we will react differently when these mistakes are made against us. We will be less inclined to take them personally (less inclined does not mean we won't get hurt) and we will be quicker to forgive.

Over the next few pages, think about the things that hurt you, and then think about the times you have done similar things to a friend. This will really help to put things in perspective.

Lullaby for Your Friend

When she's crying on your shoulder
And you don't know what to say,
Just whisper softly in her ear
That everything will be okay.
When she says her heart is broken
And her soul feels so alone,
Just tell her that you love her,
Just tell her on the phone.
When you hear her breathe so gently
And see tears fall from her eyes,
Wipe them one by one away
And keep her warm and dry.
And soon she'll look up at you
And maybe start to smile,
And thank you just for being there
Through all the painful while.
And you'll look down in her golden eyes,
And know just what to say:
That on you she can depend
And everything will be okay.

Rebecca Woolf

★ List the names you've been called, both *good* and *bad*:

1. _____
2. _____
3. _____
4. _____
5. _____
6. _____
7. _____
8. _____
9. _____
10. _____

★ Write about a time someone spread a rumor about you that was not true:

_____

_____

_____

_____

_____

_____

★ Have you ever participated in teasing or name-calling? Tell about it:

_____

_____

_____

_____

_____

_____

★ How did it feel?

_____

_____

_____

_____

_____

_____

My parents keep asking how school was.
It's like saying, "How was that drive-by shooting?"
You don't care how it was; you're lucky
to get out alive.

Angela
My So-Called Life

★ Describe a time when you felt this way about school or life:

_____

_____

_____

_____

_____

_____

_____

_____

_____

_____

A friend who is happy for you when things are going well is the best type of friend.

Christine Kalinowski

★ Are you happy for your friends when good things happen to them? Why or why not?

_____

_____

_____

★ Do you ever get jealous or envious of a friend's good fortune? If yes, give an example:

_____

_____

_____

★ Have you ever felt that a friend received praise for something when you were the one who deserved it? Describe what happened:

_____

_____

_____

Dear Kim,

I wrote this poem about the "popular" girl that is found in every school. The one that gets all the attention, and the one every other girl longs to be.

Her

There are so many things I don't understand,
And perhaps I never will,
The way they'll run to hold her hand,
Just because she's standing still.

There are so many things I don't comprehend,
And now I won't even try,
The way they can't or won't let me in,
It makes me want to cry.

But what's wrong with me? Why can't I see?
I swear I'm just the same,
My eyes will tear, my wounds will bleed,
But I don't seem to have a name.

The more they do it, the more I lose,
The more I can't escape,
The more they hurt, and the more abuse,
The less I'm able to take.

Sami Armin

★ Is there a popular girl or guy at your school whom you resent? Why?

_____

_____

_____

_____

_____

★ Do you ever feel "insignificant" or despised? When?

_____

_____

_____

_____

_____

★ Have you ever hurt so bad that you felt like you just couldn't take it anymore? Write about it:

_____

_____

_____

_____

_____

It is always best to talk things through
before reacting or jumping
to conclusions.

Kimberly Kirberger

★ Do you think talking to someone you're angry with can make things better? How?

_____

_____

_____

_____

_____

_____

_____

_____

_____

_____

_____

_____

It's much more valuable to look for
the strengths in others—you gain nothing by
criticizing people's imperfections.

Daisaku Ikeda

★ Do you tend to criticize people? Why do you think you
do this?

_____

_____

_____

_____

_____

_____

_____

_____

_____

_____

_____

_____

_____

Jealousy, Hurt and Betrayal

Jealousy, Hurt and Betrayal

Jealousy, Hurt and Betrayal

Jealousy, Hurt and Betrayal

Jealousy, Hurt and Betrayal

_____

_____

_____

_____

_____

_____

_____

_____

_____

_____

_____

_____

_____

_____

_____

_____

_____

_____

_____

_____

nine

Friends in Trouble

It is always a challenge to stick by a friend who is making choices we disagree with and are sometimes even dangerous. But it is at these times that our friends need us most.

Kimberly Kirberger

Friends in Trouble

Sometimes having someone who understands
can give others the strength to go on.

Daisaku Ikeda

When someone we love is in trouble, it is heart-wrenching. It is so hard to see them in pain and it is even harder to realize that sometimes there is not much we actually can do. This is a time when it is very important to have someone to talk to who can be objective about the situation. It is also important to write in your journal as an outlet for your frustrating feelings and a way to put things in perspective.

There are some circumstances when it is vital that you speak with an adult or a professional. If someone is causing harm to himself or herself or to someone else, you have to speak up. If someone is talking about suicide or harming another person, you definitely must speak to an adult who can take the appropriate action.

Making these choices will be more than difficult. You have to think about the long-term well-being of your friend and remember that, more often than not, when someone has had to go to an adult for help, in the end, the friend is extremely grateful.

No matter what the situation, there is only so much that you can do. You can give your friend love and support and refrain from judgment, but also remember to take care of yourself. These are hard times no matter what the problem and no matter how you choose to deal with it. It is very important that you have someone to support you and that you know the situation is essentially in God's hands.

The Night

The night that created all of my fears
That I have dreamt of every night for years.
The night that upset the entire town
Was the same night that turned my world around.
He had a drink, and had some more,
And then he staggered out the door.
We left our friends there at the bar,
And stepped into my drunk friend's car.
The night I thought my life would end
I got in the car with an ignorant friend.
It doesn't matter if they're mean or nice,
Before you get in, you'd better think twice.
They could be eighteen or thirty-five
But that doesn't mean they're okay to drive.
Today I wonder what would have been
If I had been a better friend.
He still would be here shining bright,
If I hadn't let him drive that night.

Jennifer Phillips

Friends in Trouble

★ What would you do if you found out your friend:

Was pregnant? _____

_____

_____

_____

Was suicidal? _____

_____

_____

_____

Had an eating disorder? _____

_____

_____

_____

Was a self-mutilator? _____

_____

_____

_____

Was being sexually abused? _____

_____

_____

_____

Was being physically abused? _____

_____

_____

_____

Was being hit by her boyfriend? _____

_____

_____

_____

Had a serious psychological problem? _____

_____

_____

_____

Had a serious drug problem? _____

_____

_____

★ Have you ever had a friend make choices that you disagreed with such as:

Lying? ☐ Yes ☐ No

Drug use? ☐ Yes ☐ No

Sex choices? ☐ Yes ☐ No

High-risk behavior? ☐ Yes ☐ No

★ If so, how did you handle it?

_____

_____

_____

_____

_____

★ Have you ever lost a friend because of negative choices he or she made? Describe what happened:

_____

_____

_____

_____

_____

★ Have you ever had a friend in trouble come to you for advice and you didn't know what to tell him or her? What did you do?

_____

_____

_____

_____

_____

_____

_____

????????????????????????????

★ Have you ever had to bring an adult or counselor in on a situation that a friend was going through? When?

_____

_____

_____

_____

_____

_____

_____

★ Write about a time that you worried for a friend's safety:

_____

_____

_____

_____

_____

_____

_____

_____

★ When have your friends ever worried about your safety?

_____

_____

_____

_____

_____

_____

_____

_____

★ How do you help someone who doesn't want your help or who *says* they don't want your help?

_____

_____

_____

_____

_____

_____

_____

★ Have you ever relied on a friend in a time of need? How did things work out?

_____

_____

_____

_____

_____

_____

_____

★ Do you feel that sharing a difficult time with a friend can make your friendship stronger? In what ways?

_____

_____

_____

_____

_____

_____

_____

★ When did you feel most grateful that you had a friend with whom to share your feelings?

_____

_____

_____

_____

_____

_____

_____

★ Write about the first time a friend helped you with a serious problem you were having:

_____

_____

_____

_____

_____

_____

★ What did they do that helped the most?

_____

_____

_____

_____

_____

_____

_____

_____

_____

★ Was there anything they did that you would have preferred they didn't do?

_____

_____

_____

_____

_____

_____

★ Has a friend of yours ever committed suicide?

☐ Yes   ☐ No

★ How did you deal with it?

_____

_____

_____

_____

_____

_____

_____

★ Have you ever felt suicidal? What happened?

_____

_____

_____

_____

_____

_____

_____

★ Has a friend ever told you they were thinking about hurting themselves? What did you do?

_____

_____

_____

_____

_____

_____

_____

_____

My Friends

When struggling to find myself,
Or trudging through thick mud.
When pulling out the thorns of love,
Or battling a flood.

When feeling like the world is black,
Trying to see the light.
Or feeling like a cornered mouse,
My circumstances tight.

I have been in vices and grips,
When pressures became tight.
Many times I could have surrendered,
But you taught me how to fight.

You are my ropes to grab on to,
When the foundations all collapse.
You stuck by me the whole time,
Through all of my mishaps.

You didn't have to stay with me,
to make sure my heart would mend.
But you made a choice to see me through,
and I thank you, my dear friends.

Eric Solan

Dear Friend

Write a letter to your best friend to express gratitude for a time when he or she was there for you:

Dear _____,

_____

_____

_____

_____

_____

_____

_____

_____

_____

_____

_____

_____

_____

Best Friend's Pages

★ What has been the most serious thing you have helped me to deal with?

_____

_____

_____

★ What was that like for you?

_____

_____

_____

★ Have I been there for you when you needed me?

☐ Yes   ☐ No

★ What was the most comforting thing I've said to you when you were going through a hard time?

_____

_____

_____

_____

★ Have you ever been worried for me?

☐ *Yes*   ☐ *No*

★ Have I ever made choices that you didn't agree with?

☐ *Yes*   ☐ *No*

★ How did that make you feel?

_____

_____

_____

_____

★ How could I help you the next time you are in need or have a major problem?

_____

_____

_____

_____

_____

_____

_____

★ Describe a time when I was there for you:

_____

_____

_____

_____

_____

_____

_____

_____

★ What did I do or say that made you feel better?

_____

_____

_____

_____

_____

_____

_____

_____

One of the hardest things we will ever face in a friendship is when a friend is in serious trouble and we have to decide what to do. It is a good idea to give some thought to what you would do if a friend of yours was in trouble. You are able to think more clearly when you aren't suffering, or worried or scared for a friend's life. The decision to go to an adult, for example, is a very difficult one but one that has saved many lives. If you find yourself currently in a situation where a friend is in trouble, talking about it with someone else will help you to see more clearly.

Either way, spend some time right now to think about it and remember to always look at the long term as opposed to what your immediate concerns are. Imagine your friend feeling better and thanking you for having the courage to do the difficult things that saved her or his life.

We must love our friends as
true amateurs love paintings; they have
their eyes perpetually fixed on the
fine parts, and see no others.

Madame d'Epinay

★ Do you have friends who need this from you?

□ Yes   □ No

★ Do you think there is a time when this doesn't apply? Give
an example:

_____

_____

_____

_____

_____

_____

_____

_____

Oh, the comfort, the inexpressible comfort of feeling safe with a person; having neither to weigh thoughts nor measure words but to pour them all out, just as it is, chaff and grain together, knowing that a faithful hand will take and sift them, keeping what is worth keeping, and then, with the breath of kindness blow the rest away.

George Eliot

★ We all need to know we have friends who will support us like this. List the friends you have who only see "what is worth keeping" in you:

1. _____

2. _____

3. _____

4. _____

5. _____

6. _____

7. _____

8. _____

9. _____

10. _____

♡ ♡ ♡ ♡ ♡ ♡ ♡ ♡ ♡ ♡ ♡ ♡ ♡ ♡

★ List the friends you do this for:

1. _____

2. _____

3. _____

4. _____

5. _____

6. _____

7. _____

8. _____

9. _____

10. _____

Who seeks a faultless friend
remains friendless.

Turkish Proverb

★ Are you able to hang in there with a friend whose faults are many?

☐ Yes   ☐ No

★ Do you ever turn your back on a friend when you begin to see their shortcomings?

☐ Yes   ☐ No

*Many people go far in life because
someone else thought
they could.*

John Maxwell

★ Have you ever felt like no one was on your side? Describe the situation:

_____

_____

_____

_____

_____

_____

★ Have you ever messed up and felt like everyone turned their backs on you? Write about it:

_____

_____

_____

_____

_____

_____

One person who still is able to see the good in you when you can no longer see it in yourself can turn everything around and put you back on the right path.

★ Have you ever been there for someone when you knew it made all the difference? Describe it:

_____

_____

_____

_____

_____

_____

_____

_____

_____

_____

_____

_____

_____

The Walk

Walk with me,
I need you now.
The road is dangerous here.
I'm lost along the path of life,
I really need you near.
Please, my love, just hold my hand,
Until the way is clear.
I need your strength and your support,
To take away my fear.
Walk with me,
I need you now.
I'm always there for you.
I know our love is powerful,
Together we'll make it through.
With you walking beside me,
I'm not afraid of anything new.
Walk with me,
I need you now.
The road is dangerous here.
I'm lost along the path of life,
I really need you near.

Elizabeth Waisanen

Friends in
Trouble

Friends in Trouble

_____

_____

_____

_____

_____

_____

_____

_____

_____

_____

_____

_____

_____

_____

_____

_____

_____

_____

_____

_____

_____

_____

_____

Friends in Trouble

Friends in Trouble

_____

_____

_____

_____

_____

_____

_____

_____

_____

_____

_____

_____

_____

_____

_____

_____

_____

_____

Friends in Trouble

Friends in Trouble

_____

_____

_____

_____

_____

_____

_____

_____

_____

_____

_____

_____

_____

_____

_____

_____

_____

ten

Growing Apart

We can never prepare ourselves for

the loss of a friend that we thought

would be by our side forever.

Kimberly Kirberger

Growing Apart

Goodbyes are not forever.
Goodbyes are not the end.
They simply mean I'll miss you
Until we meet again.

Kristin Pruett

Growing apart from our friends is part of growing up. We make a thousand promises that it isn't going to happen to our friendships, but hardly anyone is able to become an adult without losing a few friends along the way.

Friendships are largely based on commonalities. We like the same things, we go to the same school and we attend the same dance classes. We share things like values and lifestyles, and then one day one of us or both of us change and suddenly things are just different.

I remember betting my best friend that I would never put a boy before our friendship. At the time I believed it 100 percent. That was, until I fell in love big time and I wanted to be with him on Friday night. At first I tried to act like everything was the same, and I even gave up spending Friday nights with him. But my best friend noticed things were different and she couldn't help but notice the hour-long phone conversation I had with him under the blankets while she watched the movie we rented by herself. It turned out that the harder I tried to act like everything was still the same, the more apparent it became that it wasn't. And it wasn't just that I had a boyfriend; it was other things, too.

She wanted me to "be the way I used to be" and I was already something completely different. I was growing up. It wasn't too long before the boy bug and the "growing up" bug got her, too, but by then it was already too late. Neither of us understood the power behind change. When change starts to happen, you can't hold it back. That would be like trying to stop the waves from breaking.

When you find yourself losing a friend or growing apart from a friend, remember that it doesn't make either of you bad people and it doesn't mean you don't care. It is just part of growing up. Try to be respectful of each other and, of course, yourself. Then, just like you have to do when a big wave gets a hold of you, try to breathe, let go, relax and do your best to go with the ride.

Write as much as you can in this chapter because you will gain so much from looking back at it. This is one of those times where you just have to trust in the process and know that things will work out for the best.

Growing Apart

★ As you get older do you find that you are growing apart from any of your friends?

☐ Yes ☐ No

★ What are some issues that might cause you to grow apart from a friend?

_____

_____

_____

_____

_____

★ Have you changed a lot in the last year? ☐ Yes ☐ No

★ If yes, how have you changed?

_____

_____

_____

_____

_____

★ Do you struggle with having to let go of friends who have moved on? Describe your feelings:

_____

_____

_____

_____

_____

_____

_____

_____

★ Write about a time when growing apart from a friend worked out okay in the end:

_____

_____

_____

_____

_____

_____

_____

Freefall

I am all alone
everyone is leaving me
now I must look inside
to see the wisdom they have left me
their hope, determination, brilliance
and their dreams
they have left me their wings
now I must try to fly
solo
I wonder will anyone be there
to catch me if I fall?
I have relied on their soft cushion
many times before
I look back to a magnificent summer behind me
my memories of good times past
I look ahead to a cloudy unknown
I am unaware
yet I press on
carrying them
in the safest place
my heart.

Julie McKeon

★ Write about a time when a friend wanted to distance himself or herself from you and you didn't feel the same way. How did it make you feel?

_____

_____

_____

_____

_____

_____

_____

★ What would you do if your best friend started to grow apart from you? How would you try and keep the friendship alive?

_____

_____

_____

_____

_____

_____

_____

Dear Friend

*W*rite a letter to your friend about the changes you have been through together:

*D*ear _____,

_____

_____

_____

_____

_____

_____

_____

_____

_____

_____

_____

_____

_____

_____

_____

_____

Best Friend's Pages

★ Do you think that time has brought us closer together or further apart?

_____

★ Was there ever a time that you worried I was growing apart from you? If so, how did you deal with it?

_____

_____

_____

_____

_____

★ What do you think causes friends to grow apart?

_____

_____

_____

_____

_____

★ What can I do to help our friendship stay strong and healthy, and to let you know that I support you to grow and change?

_____

_____

_____

_____

_____

_____

_____

_____

_____

_____

_____

_____

_____

_____

My good friend Nico has a quote in this chapter where he says, "Growing apart is hard because hardly ever do friends grow apart at the same time." He is so right. If growing apart from friends happened in an organized way so that both people came to the same conclusions at the same time, a lot of pain would be spared. Sadly, this is not how it happens. One person changes or grows—or doesn't change or grow—and the other person goes through his own changes, and soon enough the friendship just isn't working anymore. The hard part, as Nico reminds us, is when the other person doesn't understand and wants the friendship to stay the same. It is so hard not to take change personally. You feel like you are no longer good enough or fun enough, and that is why your friend is moving on.

So, it is important to think about the times when you were the one to grow apart first. Think about the reasons why a friendship ended simply because. The more you can get in touch with the times when you were the one who grew out of a friendship, the more you will be okay when someone else grows apart from you.

I wanted to hug Sharon,
and tell her things, like how awful I felt,
but it was like I didn't have the right,
because we weren't friends
anymore.

Angela
My So-Called Life

★ Have you ever felt like this?

_____

_____

_____

_____

_____

_____

_____

_____

_____

_____

_____

True friendship is like sound health,
the value of it is seldom known
until it be lost.

Charles Caleb Colton

★ Have you ever lost a friend?   ☐ Yes   ☐ No

★ What happened?

_____

_____

_____

_____

_____

_____

★ How do you feel about the friendship now?

_____

_____

_____

_____

Childhood Memories

Can you come out and play again?
My life has gone askew.
I yearn for those simpler times,
And childhood memories with you.

Such a world we had to explore.
On our own little street:
Doorbell ditching and hopping walls,
Scampering on dirty bare feet.

We learned to ride our bikes,
And peddled for hours on end.
Back then we turned to our mommies
For all our problems to mend.

We went to Erin's dress-up parties,
And swam each summer day.
Until we finished junior high,
And had to go our separate ways.

Now life is changing,
So much and so fast.
I think often of our carefree times,
And long to return to the past.

Holly Hoffman

★ Does this poem make you think of a friend you've grown apart from?

□ *Yes*   □ *No*

★ Write about how you've grown apart:

_____

_____

_____

_____

_____

_____

_____

_____

_____

_____

_____

_____

_____

_____

Sharon: So you just drop your
oldest friend for no reason?
I mean, just tell me what I did.
Angela: I can't. It's not like one thing,
it's not like that.

My So-Called Life

★ Do you have a friend or friends whom you feel this way about?

☐ Yes   ☐ No

★ Are you okay with growing apart from certain people? Why or why not?

_____

_____

_____

_____

★ Are you losing friends in a similar way? Describe one:

_____

_____

_____

_____

Once I have loved someone
and called them friend, they will
always live in my heart.

Kimberly Kirberger

★ Do you have friends you have grown apart from but continue to love? Write about them:

_____

_____

_____

_____

_____

_____

_____

_____

_____

_____

Growing apart is hard because
hardly ever do friends grow apart
at the same time.

Nico Aguayo

★ Write about a time when you grew apart from a friend but
he or she wanted your friendship to stay the way it was:

_____

_____

_____

_____

_____

_____

_____

_____

_____

_____

_____

_____

Growing Apart

Growing Apart

Growing Apart

_____

_____

_____

_____

_____

_____

_____

_____

_____

_____

_____

_____

_____

_____

_____

_____

_____

_____

_____

_____

_____

_____ Growing

_____ Apart

_____

_____

_____

_____

_____

_____

_____

_____

_____

_____

_____

_____

_____

_____

_____

_____

_____

_____

_____

_____

_____

Growing Apart

_____

_____

_____

_____

_____

_____

_____

_____

_____

_____

_____

_____

_____

_____

_____

_____

_____

_____

_____

_____

eleven

To me, the best parts of friendship are

those precious moments when you're together

and you know that you are exactly where

you need to be. Your heart is full,

but completely at ease.

Kimberly Kirberger

The Best of Friendship

To laugh often and much,
to win the respect of intelligent people
and the affection of children,
to earn the appreciation of honest critics
and endure the betrayal of false friends,
to appreciate beauty,
to find the best in others,
to leave the world a bit better . . .
to know that even one life has breathed
easier because you have lived.
This is to have succeeded!

Ralph Waldo Emerson

While writing the *Friendship* book and now this journal, I have had to look very closely at myself, my friends and everything in between.

Now that I am examining the best things about friendship, I find myself drawing an interesting conclusion. When I close my eyes and go inside my heart and think about friendship, the feelings that come up are mixed. I am happy to have been blessed with great friends. I am sad because I have lost friends to death, to distance and, in some cases, because of something that one of us did wrong. But when I think about the aspects of friendship that have made me the happiest, it is the selfless acts of kindness that were given to me and given by me.

I am very grateful to my friend who came to sit by my side when my first husband was sick and was still sitting by my side even after he had passed away.

I am deeply touched every time my best friend shows up with little presents for me that have been wrapped with the utmost care.

I become absolutely giddy when I remember the incredible poem my brother wrote for me on my birthday.

There is also a certain peace that comes over me when I remember the times I was able to bring comfort to a friend who was in need. I feel good about myself because I have a friend who I have never said a bad word about. I am overjoyed because someone I love very much has found the love of his life.

I like the way I feel when I love someone unconditionally. I like the way it feels to play a part in making someone else's dreams come true.

We often find ourselves trying to define friendship in terms of what a friend can do for us. We only need to turn that definition around to find the true meaning of friendship.

Being a friend means being there . . . sometimes when you would rather be somewhere else.

Being a friend means listening rather than giving advice.

Being a friend means forgiving the small hurts and making room for the bigger kindnesses.

Being a friend means sometimes giving up a night with a boyfriend or girlfriend to be with your friend.

Being a friend means having only kind words to say about your friend.

Being a friend makes your heart warmer than even the great joy of having one.

I Found a Tiny Starfish

I found a tiny starfish
in a tidepool in the sand.
I picked up the tiny starfish
and held him in my hand.

A small and tiny starfish
hardly bigger than my thumb.
An orange and gold starfish
not belonging to anyone.

I thought that I would take him
from the tidepool by the sea
and bring him home to give to you
a gift from you to me.

But as I held the starfish
his skin began to dry.
Without his special seaside home,
my gift to you would die.

I found a tiny starfish
in a tidepool by the sea.
I hope whoever finds him next
will leave him there like me.

The gift that I have saved for you?
The best thing I could give
I found a tiny starfish
and for you I let him live.

Dayle Ann Dodds

The Best of Friendship

★ Write about something a close friend did for you that made you happy:

_____

_____

_____

_____

★ Write about an inside joke between you and a close friend:

_____

_____

_____

_____

★ Write about a time when you were happy you had a best friend to stand up for you:

_____

_____

_____

_____

★ Remember a time when you were glad you had a friend to depend on:

_____

_____

_____

_____

_____

_____

_____

_____

_____

★ Why do your friends make you happy?

_____

_____

_____

_____

_____

_____

_____

My Perfect Friend

You made me cry today
and not because you made me sad,
but because you made me laugh
and I couldn't contain my joy.
It spilled out onto my face
with every joke you told.
You are so funny.

I couldn't look at you today
and not because you looked bad,
but because every time I looked at you
I would burst out laughing.
You said something and it was all I could do
to keep from losing my drink.
It was that contagious.

You made me feel like a pauper today
and not because I have no money
but because there would never be enough
to buy you all that you deserve:
your favorite flowers and yummy-smelling candles
and your very own island where you could find
perfect peace.
You deserve it all.

ı couldn't tell you the truth today
and not because I was keeping something from you
but because the truth is that
you are so beautiful, so loving and such a perfect friend
and I felt shy expressing that to you.
I'm not always good with words.
But I think that you should know.

You made me smile today
and not because you said something nice
but because you are something nice.
And someone who brings me such joy.
And I love you for that.

Tasha Boucher

★ Make a list of the best things about friendship. Put the name of a friend you get this from next to each one.

1. _____ _____

2. _____ _____

3. _____ _____

4. _____ _____

5. _____ _____

6. _____ _____

7. _____ _____

8. _____ _____

9. _____ _____

10. _____ _____

★ What difference do your friends make in your life?

_____

_____

_____

_____

_____

_____

_____

★ What kinds of things do you and your friends do together?

_____

_____

_____

_____

_____

★ Write about the best time you ever had with a friend:

_____

_____

_____

_____

_____

★ What makes your best friend so special? If you do not have a best friend, write about why one of your close friends is so special:

♡ _____

_____

_____

_____

_____

★ What do you think is the greatest reward for being a good friend?

_____

_____

_____

_____

_____

★ What is a really nice thing you and your friends did for another friend?

_____

_____

_____

_____

★ What is the most meaningful thing a friend has ever said to you?

66 _____

_____

_____ 99

★ Write about a time when a friend made an everlasting impact on your life:

_____

_____

_____

_____

_____

_____

_____

_____

★ Write about an important lesson or concept a friend has taught you:

_____

_____

_____

_____

_____

_____

_____

_____

Dear Friend

*M*ake a list for your friend of the best moments of your friendship so far. Include the best times you've had with him or her or the best part about being his or her friend:

1. _____

2. _____

3. _____

4. _____

5. _____

6. _____

7. _____

8. _____

9. _____

10. _____

Best Friend's Pages

★ What do you value most about our friendship?

_____

_____

_____

_____

_____

★ What is the nicest thing I ever did for you?

_____

_____

_____

_____

_____

★ What do you think I like best about you?

_____

_____

_____

_____

★ Describe a time we had together that you think of as "the best":

_____

_____

_____

_____

★ Do I express well enough how much I love you and value our friendship?

☐ Yes ☐ No

★ Make a list of the things you would like us to do together:

1. _____
2. _____
3. _____
4. _____
5. _____
6. _____
7. _____
8. _____
9. _____
10. _____

Examining our friendships as closely as we have can be very difficult, but also incredibly rewarding. You will begin to see changes in yourself immediately. Things you did in the past, without even thinking about them, will now be things you think about first. Gratitude and compassion for your friends will begin to fill up more space in your heart than bitterness and distrust. You will have a deeper understanding about why people do the things they do and a deep awareness that these behaviors are not personal to you. You will not jump to conclusions as quickly, but will instead talk things through and really use the tool of communication. To put it simply, because of the work you have done in this journal, you will be able to experience more joy in your friendships.

While answering these final questions, think about how far you have come to be where you are now. Think about the people who love you and the huge capacity you have for being a good friend. Allow yourself to feel and acknowledge the love that is in your life and the friends that you share that love with. Be aware of any resistance you have to completely immersing yourself in the good stuff. Then, as a final exercise, let go of the resistance, take a few breaths and celebrate with your whole heart the incredible gift of friendship.

I shot an arrow into the air,
It fell to earth, I knew not where;
For so swiftly it flew, the sight
Could not follow it in its flight.

I breathed a song into the air,
It fell to earth, I knew not where;
For, who has sight so keen and strong
That it can follow the flight of song?

Long, long afterward, in an oak
I found the arrow, still unbroke;
And the song, from beginning to end,
I found again in the heart of a friend.

Henry Wadsworth Longfellow

★ Write a poem about friendship:

_____

_____

_____

_____

_____

_____

_____

_____

_____

_____

_____

_____

_____

_____

_____

_____

_____

_____

The One You Rely On

It's so nice to know I've got a
  hand to hold.
As the paths I choose begin to
  unfold.
Whether scary or pleasant, be it
  nightmare or dream.
In the dark of my loneliness, you
  are my sunbeam.
You took my hand when no one else
  would.
And made me feel like no other
  friend could.
In the midst of the darkness, you
  brought me the light.
When life left me grounded, you
  set me aflight.
I love you, I need you to know that
  I care.
In your hour of need, it's me who
  will be there.
Always I'll be your shoulder to
  cry on.
And forever I'll be the one you
  rely on.

Jesse Patrick

There's so many different ways
to be connected to people. There are the people
you feel this unspoken connection to, even
though there's not even a word for it.
There's the people you've known forever,
who know you in this way that other people
can't, because they've seen you change . . .
they've let you change.

Angela
My So-Called Life

★ Make a list of the friends you feel an unspoken connection
to:

1. _____

2. _____

3. _____

4. _____

5. _____

6. _____

7. _____

★ Make a list of the friends "who have known you forever" and the ones who have "let you change": *(The same person can be on both lists!)*

Friends You've Known Forever

_____

_____

_____

_____

_____

_____

_____

_____

_____

_____

_____

_____

_____

_____

_____

Friends Who Let You Change

_____

_____

_____

_____

_____

_____

_____

_____

_____

_____

_____

_____

_____

_____

_____

It's an amazing feeling—
maybe even more amazing than the feeling
I get when I perform—to be able to make
a difference in someone's life. If you can change
things for the better, if you can brighten
someone's world a little bit, you just want
to spend every moment doing it.

Britney Spears

★ Make a list of small things you have done to brighten someone else's life:

1. _____

2. _____

3. _____

4. _____

5. _____

6. _____

7. _____

8. _____

9. _____

10. _____

★ Make a list of things that have been done for you that have brightened your life:

1. _____
2. _____
3. _____
4. _____
5. _____
6. _____
7. _____
8. _____
9. _____
10. _____
11. _____
12. _____
13. _____
14. _____
15. _____

*M*ake a list of things you want to do for your friends to bring them some happiness:

For example:

Tasha: Write her a thank-you card for just being her.

Mitch: Make him a CD of his favorite dance music.

1. _____

2. _____

3. _____

4. _____

5. _____

6. _____

7. _____

8. _____

9. _____

10. _____

11. _____

12. _____

13. _____

14. _____

15. _____

Lessons from Friends

I've learned from Christine
that being myself
is the greatest gift that I can give.

I've learned from Caitlin
that not everything has to be an issue or be dramatic,
and it's okay to just have a good time.

I've learned from Charlotte
not to stress out about our future too much,
we have our whole lives to look forward to.

I've learned from Hannah
that our actions have consequences,
but they can be forgiven.

I've learned from Hayley
that we can do nothing
and still manage to have the best time.

I've learned from Amber
that it's acceptable to be in a bad mood,
but never to be cruel to the people you love.

I've learned from Vanessa
that we know just as much as our elders
because maturity is achieved by experience and not age.

I've learned from Kim
that our dreams are out there,
we just have to go find them.

I've learned from Ashley
that no matter how far away friends are,
they're always thinking about each other.

I've learned from Lily
that your oldest friends are the ones
who know you the best.

I've learned from Laura
that friends are so much more important
than any guy.

I've learned from all my friends
that they are the most important people in my life.

Jenny Sharaf

A friend who likes you teaches you to like yourself. Friends exchange the gift of self-confidence.

Carol Weston

★ Write about a time when a friend helped you to like yourself better:

_____

_____

_____

_____

_____

_____

_____

_____

_____

_____

_____

The best kind of friend is
one who can truly understand why you
are feeling the way you are.

Christine Kalinowski

★ Have you ever felt like no one understands you?

_____

_____

_____

_____

_____

★ Do you have friends who you feel truly understand you?

_____

_____

_____

_____

_____

Friendship is genuine when two
friends can enjoy each other's company
without speaking a word
to one another.

George Ebers

★ Do you think this is true? Why or why not?

_____

_____

_____

_____

★ Do you have a friend like this? If yes, write about her:

_____

_____

_____

_____

My Best Friend

Please give me direction,
When I have lost my way.
Please give me shelter,
When I have no place to stay.
Please be understanding,
For perfect I am not.
Please never stop loving me,
No matter what I do.
If you can do these things for me,
I'll do the same for you.
Please be honest and open,
Because it's okay to cry.
And know one day the time might come,
For us to say good-bye.
But no matter what, I'll cherish you,
For being my best friend.
There's nothing I wouldn't do for you,
We're friends until the end.

Teal Henderson

A friend hears the song in my heart and sings it to me when my memory fails.

Reader's Digest

★ Friends remind us of our best qualities. This is especially important when we forget. Do you remind your friends of their good qualities? In what ways?

_____

_____

_____

_____

★ Do your friends remind you of yours? How?

_____

_____

_____

★ What *are* the songs in your heart?

_____

_____

_____

Making a Difference

Staying up late at night
I ponder the future courses of my life
And appreciate the peace
Of residing in the silence of the darkness.
I reflect on my past achievements:
Not awards, nor competitions, nor championships
But times when something I did
Truly caused inspiration for someone else,
The things that someone, somewhere
Thought worthy of praise
And if for but a moment
My heart was opened and I thought maybe,
Just maybe I was worth something after all.

Allison Thorp

Often we have no time for our friends, but all the time in the world for our enemies.

Leon Uris

This is a sad, but true quote. I know I have been guilty of this many times. We seem to have more time to worry about that one person who is mean to us than we do to be grateful for all the people who are nice.

★ Do you spend more time thinking and worrying about the people who don't like you than you do being happy about the ones who do?

_____

_____

_____

_____

_____

_____

_____

_____

_____

The Best Advice

If you can see a blue patch,
In the midst of cloudy skies.
If you can find hope on the saddest of days,
A better day will rise.
If you can see a person,
For who he is deep within.
If you can judge by character,
Instead of the color of their skin.
If you can make a living,
Out of a lifelong dream.
If you can see the shine,
In the dirtiest of things.
Then you will be blessed with things in life,
That others can't enjoy.
Because you have the heart of an angel,
In the body of a boy.
In the darkest moments of life,
You'll always make it through.
Just remember to treat others,
The way you want them to treat you.

Teal Henderson

Think where man's glory
most begins and ends,
And say my glory was
I had such friends.

W.B. Yeats

★ Make a list of your friends. Next to each name write how he or she makes you a better person:

1. _____   _____

2. _____   _____

3. _____   _____

4. _____   _____

5. _____   _____

6. _____   _____

7. _____   _____

8. _____   _____

9. _____   _____

10. _____   _____

*A good friend is a connection to life—
a tie to the past, a road to the future, the key
to sanity in a totally insane world.*

Lois Wyse

★ Do you have a friend who helps to keep you sane? How does she or he do this?

_____

_____

_____

_____

_____

★ Are you that kind of friend to someone in particular? How do you keep them sane?

_____

_____

_____

_____

_____

No matter how strong you are, you can't
do everything yourself. Friends feel rejected if you
don't let them help you. Learn how to accept
favors as graciously as you offer them.

Mindy Morgenstern

★ Are you able to ask for help?   ☐ Yes   ☐ No
Why or why not?

_____

_____

_____

★ Are you uncomfortable when you have needs?

_____

_____

_____

★ Are you comfortable receiving?

_____

_____

_____

My Wish for You

You were there for me when I needed a shoulder to cry on, a person to hug and a person to talk to.

Now I am giving back to you by wishing you everything in life you need.

I wish all of your dreams to come true—and that you enjoy everything your dreams may bring to you.

I wish you happiness—for no one loves life more than a happy being.

I wish you love—the kind of love you give to others.

I wish you struggles—for struggles make you a stronger person.

I wish you strength—so you can pull yourself through the hard times.

I wish you beauty—inside and out.

I wish you confidence—every step of the way.

I wish you self-esteem—so you will know how important you are to everyone.

I wish you speech—so you can tell the world your ideas and make us a better society.

I wish you friendship—for you should always have a friend at your side.

I wish you laughter—so you can light up the world with your giggles.

I wish you energy—so you can reach the stars.

I wish you colors—for life is dull if seen in black and white.

And above all, I wish you everything your heart desires—for you are my friend, forever and always.

And if we shall drift apart—remember how important you are to me.

And how much you are loved.

Emily Kaiser

The Best of Friendship

The Best of Friendship

The Best of Friendship

_____

_____

_____

_____

_____

_____

_____

_____

_____

_____

_____

_____

_____

_____

_____

_____

_____

_____

_____

_____

The Best of Friendship

The Best of
Friendship

_____

_____

_____

_____

_____

_____

_____

_____

_____

_____

_____

_____

_____

_____

_____

_____

_____

_____

_____

_____

Who Is Kimberly Kirberger?

Kimberly is an advocate for teens, a writer for teens, a mother of a teen, and a friend and confidante to the many teens in her life. She is committed to bettering the lives of teens around the globe through her books and the outreach she does for teens on behalf of her organization, Inspiration and Motivation for Teens, Inc.

Kim's love for teens was first expressed globally with the publication of the bestselling *Chicken Soup for the Teenage Soul*. This book was a true labor of love for Kim, and the result of years of friendship and research with teens from whom she learned what really matters. After the success of the first *Teenage Soul* book, and the outpouring of hundreds and thousands of letters and submissions from teens around the world, Kim went on to coauthor the *New York Times* #1 bestsellers *Chicken Soup for the Teenage Soul II* and *Chicken Soup for the Teenage Soul III,* as well as *Chicken Soup for the Teenage Soul Journal* and *Chicken Soup for the College Soul.* Kim's empathic understanding of the issues affecting parents led her to coauthor the recent release *Chicken Soup for the Parent's Soul.*

In October 1999, the first book in Kim's *Teen Love* series was released. *Teen Love: On Relationships* has since become a *New York Times* bestseller. Her friendship and collaboration with Colin Mortensen of MTV's *Real World Hawaii* produced the much-loved *Teen Love: A Journal on Relationships* and the recently released *Teen Love: On Friendship.*

Kim lives in Southern California with her husband, John, and son, Jesse. When she is not reading letters she gets from teens, she is offering them support and encouragement in the forums on her Web site, *www.iam4teens.com.* She also enjoys nurturing her family, listening to her son's band and hanging out with her friends.

Kimberly and Colin have been speaking at high schools and middle schools, and have developed a much sought-after program for teens.

For information or to schedule Kim and Colin for a presentation, contact:

I.A.M. for Teens, Inc.
P.O. Box 936
Pacific Palisades, CA 90272
Web site: *www.iam4teens.com*

e-mail for stories: *stories@iam4teens.com*
e-mail for letters and feedback: *kim@iam4teens.com*

Contributors

Sami Armin is a biology student at the University of Western Ontario in Canada. Her hobbies include playing tennis, golf and writing poetry. Her poem is dedicated to her three best friends. She can be reached by e-mail at *gidget1358@hotmail.com*.

Christi Bergschneider has been writing poetry for six years. She enjoys writing because it helps her express her feelings. She wrote "Rose," because it was the way she was before she entered high school. She can be reached by e-mail at *criie@yahoo.com*.

Michele Booths is a sixteen-year-old student living in Pennsylvania. She writes, if not for others, for herself. Her inspiration was her grandfather who also shared the same interest. She can be reached by e-mail at *bemine14@hotmail.com*.

Tasha Boucher lives in Los Angeles and is a graduate student in the Counseling program at Cal State Northridge. She has worked as a counselor with at-risk teens and currently teaches a Creative Writing workshop to teenage girls in residential treatment. Her greatest joy has come from her relationship with an incredible teenage girl she has had the pleasure of mentoring over the past three years. Tasha can be reached at *tasha_boucher@hotmail.com*.

Alejandra Capdevila is currently a freshman in high school. She lives in Burlington, Iowa, with her parents and siblings. She can be reached by e-mail at *Ajsweety42@aol.com*.

Sara Beth Cowan is currently a senior in high school in Massachusetts. She is committed to being an individual, and writes with the intention of inspiring readers to follow her lead and to break free of the expectations of society. She can be reached by e-mail at *Little_Earthquake83@hotmail.com*.

Jessica Cox is an eighteen-year-old high-school student. She loves to read in her spare time. Her poem is dedicated to her best friends, Ariel and Nikki-Jo, and her sister, Maria.

Dayle Ann Dodds is a screenwriter and award-winning author of over fifteen books for children. Her titles include *Wheel Away!, The Color Box, Ghost and Pete, The Great Divide,* and *Sing, Sopie,* which has been animated for television. She can be reached by e-mail at *Sardines7@aol.com*.

Anne G. Fegely resides with her parents, Kathy and Jeff, and her brothers, Adam and Alex. A senior in high school, Anne enjoys sketching portraits, powerlifting and writing poetry in her leisure time. Future plans include attending college to major in English and secondary education.

Kristina Hardenbrook is seventeen years old and a junior in high school, where she has been a cheerleader for two years. She has lived in her town of Beverly all her life with her dad, Bob, her mom, Chong, her brother, Kris, and her dog, Pepper. She enjoys reading and writing poetry. This is the second time her material has been published and she is very excited. She can be reached by e-mail at *SUPRGRL134@aol.com*.

Teal Henderson is no longer with us. She died shortly after her seventeenth birthday. She embraced life fully, almost fearlessly, as if she knew her time here would be short. She was her parents' sunshine and though they no longer bask in her light, they will always feel the warmth of her love.

Holly Hoffman has decided to graduate from high school a semester early and has been accepted to Brigham Young University where she will major in nursing. She enjoys traveling with her family and snowboarding. She spends much of her time reading and writing poetry. She can be reached by e-mail at *Hoff2365@aol.com.*

Leah Houston is currently a college student. She can be reached by e-mail at *Hous1844@mail.plattsburgh.edu.*

Emily Kaiser is a high-school student in Minneapolis, Minnesota. Her poetry has also been included in local publications. Her poem is dedicated to her best friend, Shanna. She can be reached by e-mail at *lilemmaleemae@aol.com.*

Miranda Karkling is fifteen years old and attends high school in Delta, British Columbia, Canada. She can be reached by e-mail at *crazychika05@dccnet.com.*

Lisa McDonald is a member of the high-school class of 2001 in New Jersey. Besides poetry, she loves art and teaching it to younger students. Lisa sends a lot of love and thanks to her family, friends and parents for showing her how to truly be herself.

Julie McKeon is a student at Marymount College in Tarrytown, New York. She plans to major in interior design. This is her first published piece of work. She enjoys writing and spending time with her friends.

Jesse Patrick is an aspiring young journalist from Shelton, Connecticut. Currently, she is attending high school and working at the *Connecticut Post* newspaper as an editor of the *CTTeen* section. This poem is dedicated to her parents for their ongoing love and support. She can be reached by e-mail at *little_one932@hotmail.com.*

Jennie Christine Petkis is a fifteen-year-old high-school honors student in Somers, CT. She has been an avid reader and writer of poetry since elementary school. She lives with her mom, dad and brother, and she loves to spend time with her friends. She can be reached by e-mail at *Imsuchablonde22@aol.com.*

Jennifer Phillips is a high-school student in southern Illinois. She has already had some of her poetry published and is very interested in writing. In her spare time she enjoys writing, reading, soccer and taking care of animals. She someday hopes to be either a veterinarian, microbiologist, writer or artist.

Candace Schoonhoven is a bilingual high-school student in Richmond Hill, Ontario, Canada. She is majoring in the arts with hopes of becoming a successful artist. For the past six years, horseback riding has been a major part of her life. She is the proud owner of her cat, Kat. She would like to dedicate her poem to her best friend, Julie.

Megan Kimm Snook is a twenty-one-year-old native Montanan currently enrolled in an advanced writing course. She has written for several publications, most recently *Teen Love: On Friendship*. She hopes to write for children. She would like to thank her mom, dad and Cody. You can reach Megan by e-mail at *bluepool@hotmail.com*.

Eric Solan is an eighteen-year-old high-school graduate in New Jersey and now attends Seton Hall University. His poem is taken out of his high-school portfolio entitled "United Notions," and is dedicated to "The Great Mrs. Avezzano," of Lodi. For more extensive writings and poetry, e-mail him at *TOOLguy16@aol.com*.

Allison Thorp is a senior in high school where she enjoys playing volleyball, leading the National Honor Society and singing in the a capella and chamber choirs. Her additional hobbies include writing, playing the piano and hanging out with her friends. She can be reached by e-mail at *althorp@citynet.net*.

Elizabeth Waisanen is a freshman at the University of Wisconsin-Madison, studying psychology. This poem is dedicated to all her friends who have been there through the hard times. She can be reached by e-mail at *Wais333@hotmail.com*.

Rebecca Woolf is a freelance writer who has been published in *Chicken Soup for the Teenage Soul II* and *III,* as well as *Teen Love: On Relationships* and *Teen Love: On Friendship*. Rebecca is currently working on publishing her first solo book of poetry called *Broken Mirrors: A Reflective Memoir*. Rebecca has appeared as a guest on MSNBC, CBS and Fox Family, and speaks regularly to students about the importance of writing. Rebecca would like to thank Kim Kirberger for all of the brilliant opportunities she has given so selflessly. (Thank you!) To reach Rebecca, please e-mail her at *rebeccawoolf@leadthestar.com*.

 Permissions

Permissions *(continued from page iv)*

A.K.A. Friend. Reprinted by permission of Jessica Cox. ©2001 Jessica Cox.

The Oath of a True Friend. Reprinted by permission of Alejandra Capdevila. ©2001 Alejandra Capdevila.

Rose. Reprinted by permission of Christi Bergschneider. ©2000 Christi Bergschneider.

Tables Turned. Reprinted by permission of Leah Houston. ©2001 Leah Houston.

My Friend and *Lullaby for Your Friend.* Reprinted by permission of Rebecca Woolf. ©2001 Rebecca Woolf.

My Heart. Reprinted by permission of Miranda Karkling. ©2000 Miranda Karkling.

Friends. Reprinted by permission of Michele Booths. ©2001 Michele Booths.

Her. Reprinted by permission of Sami Armin. ©1998 Sami Armin.

The Night. Reprinted by permission of Jennifer Phillips. ©2001 Jennifer Phillips.

My Friends. Reprinted by permission of Eric Solan. ©2000 Eric Solan.

The Walk. Reprinted by permission of Elizabeth Waisanen. ©2001 Elizabeth Waisanen.

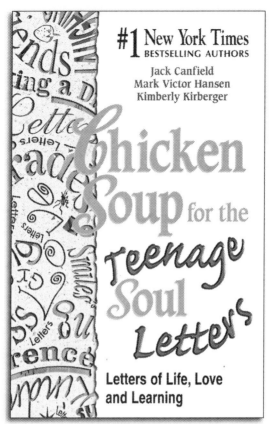

#1 New York Times
BESTSELLING AUTHORS
Jack Canfield
Mark Victor Hansen
Kimberly Kirberger

Chicken Soup for the Teenage Soul Letters

Letters of Life, Love and Learning

Code #8040 • Paperback • $12.95

A collection of the most important letters received from teens responding to the *Chicken Soup for the Teenage Soul* series, this is a powerful reflection of the feelings of a generation. Some letters will make you laugh others will make you cry but all will reveal that teens share similar outlooks, experiences and feelings.

REAL ISSUES

Code #8156 • Paperback • $12.95

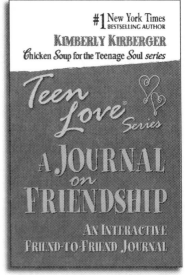

Code #9128 • Paperback • $12.95